Contents

How Changes in Immigration Policy Might Affect the Federal Budget

Summary

During the past two years, the Congress has considered proposals to modify the nation's immigration system. The Border Security, Economic Opportunity, and Immigration Modernization Act (S. 744), passed by the Senate in June 2013, addresses multiple facets of immigration policy, including changes to the existing visa system, improvements in border security and law enforcement, and changes to the status of people who currently live in the country without legal authorization. Other proposals have focused on one component of immigration policy—for example, improving border security or changing certain aspects of the visa system. Whether the proposals involve broad or narrow changes to immigration policy, they could have a variety of consequences for both citizens and noncitizens, for the federal government, and for state and local governments. This Congressional Budget Office (CBO) report examines some of those proposals and how such changes would affect the federal budget.

When estimating the budgetary consequences of immigration reform, CBO considers various factors. Depending on the details of proposed legislation, changes to immigration policy could have a significant effect on the size and composition of the noncitizen population and, as a result, on rates of participation in federal programs and the payment of taxes. For that reason, when estimating the budgetary effects of proposals, CBO considers the demographic and labor force characteristics of foreign-born people, their eligibility for and participation in federal programs, their tax liability, changes in the economy, and a number of other factors. If proposals were combined into a single, more comprehensive immigration bill, estimates of the budgetary effects would take into account the complex interactions among the various provisions; the net effect would not be a simple summation of the individual effects.

What Are the Demographic and Labor Force Characteristics of Noncitizens?

Of the 41 million foreign-born people living in the United States in 2012, about 22 million were non-citizens—a category that includes lawful permanent residents, or LPRs (people who have been granted permanent admission to the United States and are eligible to live and work here); temporary residents and visitors; and unauthorized residents.[1] About half of those non-citizens were LPRs, temporary residents, or visitors; the rest, between 11 million and 12 million people, were in the country without authorization, a number that has changed little over the past few years.

Noncitizens differ from both foreign- and native-born citizens across several demographic dimensions, especially in terms of their skills and employment status. In particular, noncitizens are much more likely to be of working age (between 25 and 64 years old) and much less likely to be 65 years old or older. They are also significantly more likely than citizens to have less than a high school diploma or GED but about as likely to have a master's or more advanced degree, reflecting a broad spectrum of education and skills. Since 1995, the unemployment rate among noncitizens has been, on average, more than a percentage point higher than that for citizens; in 2013, the unemployment rate for noncitizens was 7.1 percent compared with 6.0 percent for citizens.

How Have Recent Administrative Actions Affected Unauthorized Residents?

The Administration has taken a number of steps to delay possible removal proceedings for unauthorized residents under a process known as deferred action. Those who are approved for deferred action are considered lawfully

---

1. See the glossary on page 35 for details about key terms used in this report.

present in the country for a limited period of time but do not gain legal status; they can, and most do, receive authorization to work.

As of September 30, 2014, about 610,000 people who entered the United States as children had been approved for deferred action through the Deferred Action for Childhood Arrivals program. In November 2014, the President expanded that program to include additional people who arrived as children and also established a deferred action program for parents of U.S. citizens and LPRs. CBO estimates that, by 2017, between 2 million and 2½ million people will have received approval for deferred action.

What Federal Benefits Can Noncitizens Receive and What Taxes Do They Pay?

Under current law, only qualified aliens—primarily comprising LPRs, refugees, and people who have been granted asylum—and some types of temporary residents are eligible to participate in most federal benefit programs, provided they meet other program-specific eligibility requirements. (For some programs, those requirements include waiting periods of several years following the attainment of qualified alien status). Some noncitizens who are not qualified aliens but are lawfully present (for example, people who have been approved for deferred action) are eligible to receive Social Security and Medicare benefits if they qualify on the basis of their age and work history. Other noncitizens are not eligible to receive benefits from most federal programs; exceptions include emergency health care services provided through Medicaid, some benefits through the Children's Health Insurance Program (CHIP), and some refundable tax credits. However, noncitizens' U.S.–born children are eligible for the same federal benefits that are available to other U.S. citizens. (See Table 1 for an overview of the eligibility requirements for noncitizens.)

Most noncitizens who live and work in the United States are subject to taxation—including income taxes, payroll taxes, excise taxes, and estate and gift taxes. The specific taxes for which they are liable, and in some cases the amount of those taxes, depend on the type of visa they hold and how long they have been in the country.

How Might Proposals to Modify the Immigration System Affect the Federal Budget?

Proposals to modify U.S. immigration policy vary greatly in scope and their potential impact on the federal budget. In this report, CBO discusses the possible effects that changes to immigration policy would have on several major federal spending programs and on federal tax revenues. Among the programs and benefits that could be affected:

■ Health care programs for low-income people— including Medicaid, CHIP, and subsidies for health insurance (which include premium and cost-sharing assistance for health insurance purchased through the exchanges that were established in 2014 under the Affordable Care Act, or ACA),[2]

■ The Supplemental Nutrition Assistance Program (SNAP),

■ Social Security,

■ Supplemental Security Income (SSI),

■ Medicare,

■ Pell grants and federal student loans,

■ Unemployment insurance, and

■ Refundable tax credits.

Each program has its own set of eligibility rules and criteria, which determine how changes to federal immigration policy would affect participation in the program and spending by the government. Consequently, such policy changes could affect spending in varying ways both in the near term and over time. Spending for some programs would change almost immediately upon enactment if more noncitizens were allowed to enter the country, whereas spending for other programs would not change much for a while: For example, under some proposals, foreign-born people who entered the country lawfully

---

2. As referred to in this report, the ACA comprises the Patient Protection and Affordable Care Act (Public Law 111-148) and the health care provisions of the Health Care and Education Reconciliation Act of 2010 (P.L. 111-152), as affected by subsequent judicial decisions, statutory changes, and administrative actions.

Table 1.

Noncitizens' Eligibility for Federal Programs

	LPRs, Refugees, and People Granted Asylum	Temporary Residents	Unauthorized Residents
Health Care for Low-Income People			
Medicaid	Only emergency services for the first five years, with some state exceptions for children and pregnant women during those first five years	Emergency services	Emergency services
CHIP	Full coverage for qualified aliens after five years, with some state exceptions for fewer than five years	State option for coverage of prenatal care, labor and delivery, and postpartum care	State option for coverage of prenatal care, labor and delivery, and postpartum care
Premium and cost-sharing assistance[a]	Eligible	Eligible	Not eligible
SNAP	LPRs under the age of 18, refugees, and people granted asylum are immediately eligible; other LPRs must wait five years	Not eligible	Not eligible
Social Security	Eligible	Eligible	Not eligible[b]
SSI	Refugees and people granted asylum are eligible on entrance; LPRs must wait five years and have 40 quarters of work credit	Not eligible	Not eligible
Medicare	Eligible	Eligible	Not eligible[b]
Pell Grants and Federal Student Loans	Eligible, no five-year wait	Not eligible	Not eligible
Unemployment Insurance	Eligible	Temporary residents with work authorization only	Not eligible
Refundable Tax Credits	Eligible	Depends on visa, home country, and amount of time in the United States	To receive, a taxpayer must generally fiile his or her tax return and have either a Social Security number or an ITIN.[b]

Source: Congressional Budget Office.

Notes: In addition to those eligibility requirements stated in the table, people must also meet the usual eligibility requirements for each program.

LPR = lawful permanent resident; CHIP = Children's Health Insurance Program; SNAP = Supplemental Nutrition Assistance Program; SSI = Supplemental Security Income; ITIN = individual taxpayer identification number.

a. Part of the Affordable Care Act, which comprises the Patient Protection and Affordable Care Act (Public Law 111-148) and the health care provisions of the Health Care and Reconciliation Act of 2010 (P.L. 111-152), as affected by subsequent judicial decisions, statutory changes, and administrative actions.

b. Formerly unauthorized residents who receive approval for "deferred action"—that is, any removal proceedings initiated against them are delayed for a period of time—are considered lawfully present without legal status. They are eligible to receive Medicare and Social Security benefits, assuming they meet the programs' requirements. In addition, unauthorized residents who are approved for deferred action and receive work authorization have Social Security numbers and therefore can claim the earned income tax credit, if they qualify.

after the policy change was implemented would auto- matically be eligible for emergency Medicaid benefits and subsidies for health insurance purchased through exchanges; they also would begin paying income and pay- roll taxes as soon as they entered the country. In contrast, additional spending for Social Security and Medicare would occur mostly after the first few decades, once new entrants had been in the workforce for a sufficient time and reached the age at which they were eligible to claim benefits.

Because most noncitizens who live and work in the United States are subject to taxation, changes to federal immigration policy would affect the amount of revenues the government collects. How total revenues collected by the federal government would change under new immi- gration policy would depend on the resulting changes in the size of the U.S. population, the types of people who would be permitted to work under those new laws, and other considerations. A policy that led to a significant increase in the working-age population would expand the labor force and lead to a significant amount of additional revenues from income and payroll taxes.

This report does not address in detail how a change in immigration policy might affect federal spending or tax revenues through its effects on the broader economy—as evidenced in changes to gross domestic product, employ- ment, and total wages. In some instances, when those effects would probably be significant, CBO and the staff of the Joint Committee on Taxation (JCT) have relaxed the long-standing convention of not incorporating such macroeconomic effects in cost estimates. Immigration legislation also could have a broader set of effects on out- put and income that are not reflected in cost estimates. Those additional economic effects include changes in the productivity of labor and capital, the income earned by capital, the rate of return on capital (and therefore the interest rate on government debt), and the differences in wages for workers with different skills. Those effects and their estimated consequences for the federal budget have, on occasion, been discussed in separate reports regarding the proposed legislation.

Earlier this month, the House of Representatives adopted a rule that requires CBO and JCT to include the budget- ary feedback of any macroeconomic effects in cost esti- mates for some major pieces of legislation.[3] Legislation that would make significant changes in immigration policy might be covered by this rule; if so, future cost

estimates provided to the House for such legislation will, to the extent practicable, incorporate the sorts of effects described here.

Because immigration proposals could affect both spend- ing and revenues, some might result in net budgetary savings whereas others might result in net budgetary costs. However, assessing the net effect on the federal budget of changes in immigration policy is complicated by a variety of factors, including a lack of reliable data about the number of unauthorized residents currently in the country and the extent to which LPRs, temporary residents, and unauthorized residents use government programs.

This report focuses on proposals that would change the status or composition of three populations of noncitizens: LPRs, temporary workers, and currently unauthorized residents.

Changing the Criteria for Admitting Lawful Permanent Residents. According to government estimates, about 13 million people currently live in the country as LPRs. Changes to visa policies that broadly affected the charac- teristics of new LPRs—for example, by shifting the type of permanent visas awarded from family-based prefer- ences to work-related or merit-based preferences— might have a significant impact on the demographic composition of LPRs and, as a result, on their use of federal programs and payment of taxes.

Under current law, permanent residents who meet program requirements are generally eligible to receive benefits after a specified waiting period or period of employment; thus, an increase in the number of LPRs would ultimately increase spending for programs such as Social Security and Medicare. Whether those residents qualify for certain means-tested benefits (such as those provided by Medicaid and SNAP) is determined, in part, by their income. If the policy change resulted in more LPRs with sufficiently low income to qualify for benefits, costs for those federal programs also would increase. In the first five years, the biggest impact on spending would

---

3. See section 2(c) of H. Res. 5, adopted on January 6, 2015, which added clause 8 to Rule XIII. The rule defines major legislation to include bills that would have a gross budgetary effect (before incorporating macroeconomic effects) in a fiscal year equal to or greater than 0.25 percent of GDP—or legislation so designated by certain committee chairmen. However, the rule does not apply to appropriation bills.

probably involve the health insurance subsidies; after that, changes in spending for other programs would have increased importance. Tax revenues also would change if the visa system was altered, though whether revenues increased or decreased would depend on the details of the policy.

Changes that significantly increased the net flow of foreign-born workers into the United States, and therefore increased the total population, would lead to an increase in the supply of labor, which would have broad effects on the economy and the budget. The magnitude of those effects would depend on factors such as the new immigrants' rate of participation in the labor force, their unemployment rate, the average number of hours they work, and their average wage.

Changing the Visa System for Temporary Workers. The United States issued about 9.2 million visas for temporary admission in 2013. About 670,000 of those visas were issued to temporary workers and the rest were issued to other temporary residents and visitors. Because temporary workers are generally not eligible to receive benefits from most federal programs, policies that changed the number of temporary visas awarded to foreign-born workers might have a smaller effect on the federal budget than changes to the number of permanent residents. However, if a temporary-worker program allowed participants to eventually adjust their status, and the number of LPRs or citizens increased as a result, the long-term fiscal impact of those residents and their children might be significant. A policy that modified the visa system in a way that resulted in a shift in the demographic composition of temporary workers also would affect the federal budget. For example, a shift that resulted in a larger share of people with more skills or education would probably reduce spending on needs-based programs and boost wages and tax revenues.

Granting Legal Status to Unauthorized Residents. Granting legal status to some or all of the noncitizens living in the country without authorization would affect their tax liability, their eligibility for federal benefits, and the amount of benefits they received. Those effects would depend critically on the specific provisions of the legislation, which would determine when and how those newly authorized residents became eligible for federal benefits. Over time, such changes in status might increase spending for a variety of federal benefits, including those provided by health care programs for low-income people

(specifically, Medicaid, CHIP, and subsidies for the purchase of health insurance through the exchanges established by the ACA), SNAP, Social Security, Medicare, and refundable tax credits. Several other federal programs, such as SSI, Pell grants, and unemployment insurance also could experience spending increases. In addition, legalization policies might result in increased tax revenues, stemming mostly from taxes on higher wages that workers may earn as a result of attaining legal status and taxes from increased reporting of employment income by workers who are currently not paying taxes.

The effects also would vary over time: In the first decade after enactment, the amount that the federal government spent on benefit programs might not rise significantly if waiting periods for benefits remained the same as they are under current law and if other eligibility rules were not changed. In subsequent years, government spending would rise as people crossed those thresholds and became eligible for benefits as they aged (for example, Social Security and Medicare benefits). In addition, children born in the United States to those residents would be eligible for benefit programs on the same basis as other citizens.

How Might Increased Enforcement of Immigration Law Affect the Federal Budget?

Proposals to enhance the enforcement of immigration law generally focus on improving border security and internal enforcement (the process of identifying, locating, and removing people who entered the country unlawfully or remained after their authorized stay had ended), or on improving the system that allows employers to verify the legal status of new workers.

Bolstering border security and improving internal enforcement could require additional federal funding for personnel—more Border Patrol agents, for instance—or more funding for improved border infrastructure and technologies. Budgetary effects also would include reductions in spending for federal benefit programs and in receipts of tax revenues that stemmed from a decrease in the number of people living in the country without authorization.

Policies designed to improve verification of a person's legal status at the workplace would target the estimated 8 million unauthorized residents who work. Some of those people have received or will receive an authorization to work under the Administration's deferred action programs. The remaining workers do so without authorization, despite requirements for newly hired workers to have evidence of work authorization and identity.

Implementing such proposals might have a significant impact on the federal budget. Expanding the existing E-Verify program would increase administrative costs of the Department of Homeland Security (DHS) and the Social Security Administration (SSA), the agencies responsible for managing the program. Such an expansion might result in lower federal revenues if more unauthorized workers were paid outside of the tax system.

Characteristics of Noncitizens

Over 41 million foreign-born people lived in the United States in 2012, making up about 13 percent of the 314 million U.S. residents that year—the largest share since 1920. Of that foreign-born population, 19 million were naturalized citizens (foreign-born people who have fulfilled the requirements of U.S. citizenship). Twenty-two million were noncitizens (a category that includes foreign-born people authorized to be in the United States, either on a temporary or permanent basis, as well as people who are not authorized to be in the United States). About half of those noncitizens were legally authorized to live or work in the United States.

Foreign-born people can gain legal entry into the United States by qualifying for a temporary stay, such as for work or education, or by qualifying for a permanent stay. They can qualify for a permanent stay by demonstrating a family relationship with a current U.S. citizen or lawful permanent resident, by meeting employment requirements, or by being granted asylum or status as a refugee. Those in the country illegally include people who originally entered without authorization as well as those who remain in the country after such authorization has expired.

Citizens and noncitizens differ in terms of demographics and participation in the labor force. Noncitizens are more likely than citizens to be of working age—between 25 and 64 years old—but they also tend to have less education (see Table 2). Male noncitizens are more likely than male citizens to be in the labor force, but the opposite is true for women. Between 2008 and 2013, the unemployment rate for noncitizen workers between the ages of 25 and 64 was more than a percentage point higher than that for workers who were citizens.

Categories of Noncitizens

The noncitizen population comprises three categories: lawful permanent residents, temporary residents and visitors, and unauthorized residents.[4]

Lawful Permanent Residents. LPRs are granted permanent admission to the United States and receive a document, commonly known as a green card, certifying that status. They are eligible to live and work in the United States, own property, and join the armed forces. Most may apply for U.S. citizenship after five years.[5] In 2013, the United States granted LPR status to 1.0 million people.

Permanent admission can be granted to noncitizens on the basis of any of the following broad criteria:

- Family relationships:

  - Immediate relatives of U.S. citizens—for example, spouses, parents and unmarried children under the age of 21;

---

4. For more details on these different types of noncitizens, see Congressional Budget Office, *A Description of the Immigrant Population—2013 Update* (May 2013), www.cbo.gov/publication/44134, and *Immigration Policy in the United States: An Update* (December 2010), www.cbo.gov/publication/21921. In this report, unauthorized residents include those who have been approved for deferred action; they are lawfully present without legal status for the duration of their deferral.

5. Estimates of the number of people granted LPR status on an annual basis are from Randall Monger and James Yankay, *U.S. Lawful Permanent Residents: 2013* (Department of Homeland Security, Office of Immigration Statistics, May 2014), http://go.usa.gov/eDeA (PDF, 267 KB). For a discussion of undercounts of the noncitizen population in the ACA data set, see Michael Hoefer, Nancy Rytina, and Bryan Baker, *Estimates of the Unauthorized Immigrant Population Residing in the United States: January 2011* (Department of Homeland Security, Office of Immigration Statistics, March 2012), http://go.usa.gov/Zs9J. The number of LPRs, legal temporary workers, and unauthorized residents may not sum to the total noncitizen population because of differences in data sets. (For example, for this report, CBO obtained data on LPRs and unauthorized populations from DHS and data on the noncitizen population from the Census Bureau's American Community Survey.) Other differences are attributable to variations in methodology and probable undercounts of the noncitizen population.

Table 2.

Demographic Characteristics of Citizens and Noncitizens, 2012

	Percentage of Total		Number of People (Millions)	
	Citizens	Noncitizens	Citizens	Noncitizens
Age Distribution				
Under the age of 25	34	19	101	4
Ages 25 to 64	51	74	150	16
Age 65 or older	15	7	43	1
Total	100	100	294	22
Women Currently or Formerly Married[a]				
Ages 15 to 24	8	17	2	*
Ages 25 to 34	53	66	10	2
Educational Attainment, Ages 25 to 64				
Less than high school diploma or GED	9	39	13	6
High school diploma or GED	27	23	40	4
Some college or associate's degree	32	15	48	2
Bachelor's degree	21	13	31	2
Master's degree or more	11	10	17	2
Total	101	99	150	16
Labor Force Participation Rate, Ages 25 to 64				
Men	82	89	61 [b]	7 [b]
Women	73	60	56 [b]	5 [b]
Total	78	75	116 [b]	12 [b]
Total	93	7	294	22
Memorandum:				
Fertililty Rates of Women, Ages 15 to 49[c]	1.8	2.3	n.a.	n.a.
Median Earnings in 2010, Ages 25 to 64 (Dollars)[d]				
Male Workers	45,000	26,000	n.a.	n.a.
Female Workers	31,700	18,200	n.a.	n.a.
All Workers	38,000	23,400	n.a.	n.a.

Source: Congressional Budget Office based on data from the Census Bureau.

Notes: Demographic information presented here is based on data from the Census Bureau's 2013 American Community Survey as extracted from the Minnesota Population Center's Integrated Public Use Microdata Series. Unemployment information is based on data from outgoing rotation groups of the Census Bureau's monthly Current Population Survey, January 1994 to December 2013.

　　　* = less than 500,000; n.a. = not applicable.

a.   Consists of all women who are married, divorced, separated, or widowed.

b.   Refers to the number of people participating in the labor force.

c.   The expected number of births experienced by a woman in a particular age range if, at each age within the range, the likelihood that she gave birth was equal to the share of women at the same age who bore a child during the survey year.

d.   Calculated for individuals between the ages of 25 and 64 with positive earnings.

- Family-sponsored preferences—for example, married and unmarried sons and daughters of U.S. citizens, spouses and dependent children of LPRs, and siblings of adult U.S. citizens.

■ Employment-based preferences—for workers with specific job skills.

■ Eligibility for the Diversity Immigrant Visa Program—a lottery-based system for people from countries with low rates of immigration to the United States.

■ Humanitarian reasons—for refugees or people who have been granted asylum, who may then apply for LPR status one year later.[6]

In 2013, about two-thirds of the new LPRs received that status on the basis of a family relationship with a U.S. citizen or LPR.

Temporary Residents and Visitors. Temporary admission to the United States is granted to foreign-born people who seek entry for a limited time and for a specific purpose, such as tourism, diplomacy, or study. In addition, people may be permitted into the United States to work for a limited time. Foreign-born people with temporary visas are generally not eligible for citizenship, and to remain in the United States on a permanent basis they would be required to apply for permanent admission.

The United States issued about 9.2 million visas for temporary admission in 2013, 58 percent more than the number issued in 2009. Visitors accounted for 81 percent of those visas; about 12 percent were issued to temporary residents such as students and their families; and temporary workers and their families accounted for about 7 percent. Much of the increase was attributable to tourist visas, perhaps because the global recession had begun to moderate by 2012.[7]

---

6. Many comprehensive immigration reform bills in recent years have focused on the broader categories of lawful immigration or unauthorized residents but have not typically called for changes in humanitarian immigration; however, S. 744 included provisions that would change the rules applying to that category. Changes to humanitarian immigration are often addressed in other bills.

7. Based on data from Department of State, Bureau of Consular Affairs, *Report of the Visa Office 2013*, Table XVI(B), http://go.usa.gov/eDJC (PDF, 147 KB).

Unauthorized Residents. DHS estimates that between 11 million and 12 million U.S. residents were in the country without authorization in 2012.[8] Unauthorized residents either enter the country illegally or stay beyond the time allowed by a visa. Nearly half of the unauthorized residents in the U.S. are believed to have originally entered the country legally.[9] The estimates suggest that the total number of unauthorized residents has risen by about 3 million since 2000. Some unauthorized residents have been approved for deferred action (see Box 1). Those residents are lawfully present without legal status.

Demographic Characteristics of Noncitizens
As a group, noncitizens differ in several important ways from citizens—whether naturalized or native born—in terms of age, marital status, fertility, and educational attainment. Those characteristics in part determine citizens' and noncitizens' eligibility for and participation in certain government programs. Therefore, such information, including when noncitizens become citizens, is important to CBO's estimates of the budgetary effects of immigration policy proposals.[10]

Age. Compared with the citizen population, a relatively small share of noncitizens are under the age of 25 or

---

8. DHS arrived at its estimate by calculating the difference between the total foreign-born population and the authorized foreign-born population. For those estimates, see Bryan Baker and Nancy Rytina, *Estimates of the Unauthorized Immigrant Population Residing in the United States: January 2012* (Department of Homeland Security, Office of Immigration Statistics, March 2013), http://go.usa.gov/eDS3 (PDF, 194 KB). The numbers that form the basis of DHS's estimate, however, came from a variety of sources, and they involved various assumptions. Moreover, because they do not reflect actual population counts, the resulting estimates are subject to considerable uncertainty. The Pew Hispanic Center also estimates the number of unauthorized workers in the United States; its most recent estimate for 2012 is about 200,000 lower than the estimate by DHS. See Jeffrey S. Passel, D'Vera Cohn, and Molly Rohal, *Unauthorized Immigrant Totals Rise in 7 States, Fall in 14* (Pew Hispanic Center, November 18, 2014), http://tinyurl.com/nf9mwzf (PDF, 2.33 MB).

9. Pew Hispanic Center, *Modes of Entry for the Unauthorized Population* (May 2006), http://tinyurl.com/korn9w9.

10. Demographic information presented here is based on data from the Census Bureau's 2013 American Community Survey as extracted from the Minnesota Population Center's Integrated Public Use Microdata Series. Unemployment information is based on data from outgoing rotation groups of the Census Bureau's monthly Current Population Survey, January 1994 to December 2013.

Box 1.

Unauthorized Residents and Deferred Action

In some cases, the Department of Homeland Security (DHS) delays removal proceedings for unauthorized residents under a process known as deferred action. Those who are approved for deferred action are considered lawfully present in the country but do not gain legal status. They can, and most do, receive authorization to work. Because they are lawfully present during the period of their deferred status, they are eligible to receive Medicare and Social Security benefits if they meet the programs' requirements. In addition, those individuals who are approved for deferred action and receive work authorization have Social Security numbers and therefore can claim the earned income tax credit if they qualify. They are ineligible for other federal benefit programs.

Childhood Arrivals. In August 2012, DHS began accepting and processing applications for deferred action from some unauthorized residents who did not yet have removal proceedings initiated against them. To qualify for this program, known as the Deferred Action for Childhood Arrivals (DACA) program, people had to meet several requirements: they must have been under 31 years of age as of June 15, 2012; been younger than 16 when they came to the United States; continuously resided in the United States since June 15, 2007; been registered in and attending school, or have graduated from high school or earned a GED; or had been honorably discharged from the military. Deferred action was granted for two years and could be renewed. The Migration Policy Institute estimates that about 2.1 million unauthorized residents may be eligible for DACA as implemented since 2012.[1] As of September 30, 2014, DHS had received about 700,000 initial applications and approved about 630,000 requests, including about 22,000 renewals of status.[2]

On November 20, 2014, the President announced a series of changes to immigration policy, including

expanding DACA.[3] That executive action expands the DACA population in two ways. It allows people who are 31 years and older and arrived in the United States as children, and unauthorized residents who meet the other DACA requirements but who arrived between June 15, 2007, and January 1, 2010, to apply for deferred action. Those two groups were excluded from the original DACA program. In addition, the November action extended the duration of deferred action from two years under previous Administration policy to three years.

The Congressional Budget Office (CBO) estimates that in 2017 there will be about 600,000 people in the country approved for deferred action as a result of the initial DACA program and about another 150,000 people approved for deferred action as a result of the expanded eligibility.

Parents of U.S. Citizens and Lawful Permanent Residents. The executive actions announced on November 20, 2014, also allow parents of U.S. citizens and lawful permanent residents to apply for deferred action if they meet the following criteria: they have been continuously present in the country since January 1, 2010; were physically present in the country on November 20, 2014, and at the time of application; had no legal status on November 20, 2014; and are not an enforcement priority for DHS. CBO estimates that in 2017 there will be about 1.5 million parents of U.S. citizens or lawful permanent residents in the country approved for deferred action as a result of the new policy.

---

1. Jeanne Batalova, Sarah Hooker, and Randy Capps, *DACA at the Two-Year Mark: A National and State Profile of Youth Eligible and Applying for Deferred Action* (Migration Policy Institute, August 2014), http://tinyurl.com/nq6kapo (PDF, 4.92 MB).

2. Citizenship and Immigration Services, "Consideration of Deferred Action for Childhood Arrivals, by Fiscal Year, Quarter, Intake, Biometrics, and Case Status, 2012 to 2014" (November 21, 2014), http://go.usa.gov/eWrk (PDF, 131 KB).

3. Jeh Charles Johnson, Secretary, Department of Homeland Security, memorandum about exercising prosecutorial discretion with respect to individuals who came to the United States as children and with respect to certain individuals who are the parents of U.S. citizens or permanent residents (November 20, 2014), http://go.usa.gov/eWrz (PDF, 3 MB).

over 65. In 2012, about one-fifth of the noncitizen population was under age 25, compared with about one-third of the citizen population (see Table 2 on page 7). In that year, only 7 percent of noncitizens were at least 65 years old, less than half the share among citizens. In contrast, nearly three-quarters of the noncitizen population was of working age (between 25 and 64 years old), compared with about half of the citizen population. According to DHS, most of the unauthorized residents were between 25 and 54 years old in 2012—about three-quarters of the unauthorized population were in that age group, compared with about half of citizens.[11]

Marital Status and Fertility. Marriage and fertility rates are generally higher among young female noncitizens than among their citizen counterparts. In 2012, 17 percent of female noncitizens ages 15 to 24 were or had been married, roughly double the share of female citizens; about two-thirds of female noncitizens ages 25 to 34 were or had been married, compared with just over half of female citizens. (The available data do not permit a reliable estimate of the percentage of marriages in which one spouse is an unauthorized resident.) The fertility rate—the expected number of births—among female noncitizens between the ages of 15 and 49 was 2.3, compared with a fertility rate of 1.8 for female citizens in the same age range.

Educational Attainment. Noncitizens' educational attainment also differs considerably from that of citizens. In 2012, about 40 percent of the noncitizen population between the ages of 25 and 64 had less than a high school diploma or GED, more than four times the share of the citizen population. A similar share of citizens and noncitizens had a high school diploma or GED, but citizens were much more likely than noncitizens to have at least some college education (64 percent compared with 38 percent).

Labor Market Characteristics of Noncitizens

Male noncitizens are more likely, and female noncitizens less likely, than their citizen counterparts to be in the labor force. Overall, the unemployment rate for non-

citizens tends to be higher than for citizens, and earnings for noncitizens tend to be lower.

Labor Force Participation. In 2012, a slightly greater share of citizens ages 25 to 64 participated in the labor force than did noncitizens in that age group, but there were significant differences between men and women. In that year, the labor force participation rate among male noncitizens was about 7 percentage points higher than among male citizens. By contrast, the labor force participation rate among female noncitizens was about 13 percentage points lower than among female citizens.[12]

Unemployment Rate. Unemployment rates vary over time with economic conditions. Nevertheless, over the past two decades, the unemployment rate has been consistently higher for noncitizen workers than it has been for citizen workers (see Figure 1). During that period, economic fluctuations resulted in larger changes in the unemployment rate among noncitizens than among citizens. The unemployment rate for noncitizens declined more than that for citizens between 1995 and 2000 and again between 2003 and 2006, when the economy was growing quickly. Conversely, the unemployment rate for noncitizen workers rose more than the rate for citizen workers between 2000 and 2003, when the economy was shrinking or growing slowly. And between 2006 and 2010, the unemployment rate among noncitizen workers between the ages of 25 and 64 rose by about 5.7 percentage points—from 4.2 percent to 9.9 percent—compared with a 4.6 percentage-point increase among citizen workers.

At least four factors contributed to the changes in employment experienced by noncitizens in recent years: a disproportionate decrease in employment in the construction sector because of the decline in the housing market; the fact that job losses among those with less education occurred at a faster rate than was the case for people with greater educational attainment; variations in local labor markets resulting from changes in demand for

---

11. Estimates of the unauthorized population are from Bryan Baker and Nancy Rytina, *Estimates of the Unauthorized Immigrant Population Residing in the United States: January 2012* (Department of Homeland Security, Office of Immigration Statistics, March 2013), http://go.usa.gov/eDS3 (PDF, 673 KB).

12. See Congressional Budget Office, *A Description of the Immigrant Population—2013 Update* (attachment to a letter to the Honorable Paul Ryan, May 8, 2013), www.cbo.gov/publication/44134, *A Description of the Immigrant Population: An Update* (June 2011), Exhibit 14, www.cbo.gov/publication/41453, and *The Role of Immigrants in the U.S. Labor Market: An Update* (July 2010), www.cbo.gov/publication/21656.

Figure 1.

Unemployment Rates Among Citizens and Noncitizens Ages 25 to 64, 1994 to 2013

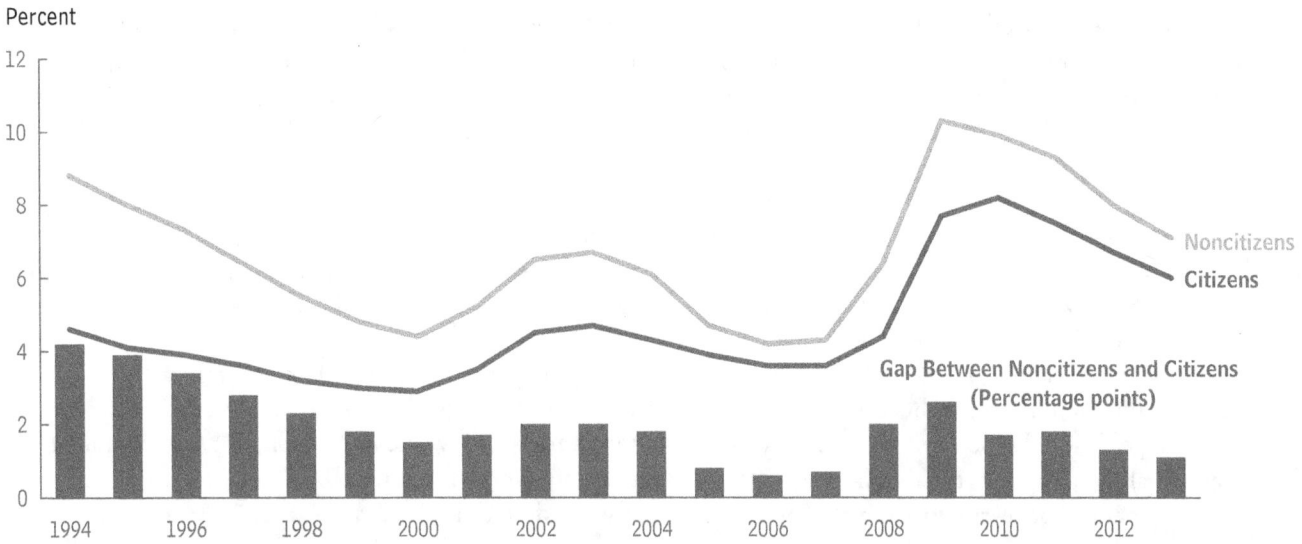

Source: Congressional Budget Office based on data from outgoing rotation groups of the Census Bureau's monthly Current Population Survey, January 1994 to December 2013, www.census.gov/cps.

certain kinds of jobs; and changes in the number and types of noncitizens in the country.

Since the end of the recent recession, the gap between the unemployment rates has narrowed, but it is still larger than it was before the recession. For citizens, the unemployment rate declined from 8.2 percent in 2010 to 6.0 percent in 2013. Among the noncitizen population, the unemployment rate fell from 9.9 percent in 2010 to 7.1 percent in 2013.

Annual Earnings. Disparities between the annual earnings of noncitizen and citizen workers can be attributed to differences in age, educational attainment, labor force participation, and the concentration of workers in particular occupational groups. In 2012, median earnings among male citizens were about 75 percent greater than those of male noncitizens; female citizens also earned about 75 percent more than their noncitizen counterparts.

Noncitizens' Eligibility for Federal Benefits and Their Tax Liability

Changes to federal immigration policy would affect the number of people eligible for federal benefits, the number of beneficiaries who participate in a variety of federal programs, and the amount of taxes people pay. Such

changes might occur through policies that modified the current visa system and altered the number of people legally admitted to the country or policies that offered unauthorized residents legal status.

Under current law, only certain noncitizens referred to collectively as qualified aliens—primarily LPRs, refugees, and people who have been granted asylum—are eligible for many public benefit programs.[13] (Most other types of noncitizens—temporary workers, visitors, and all unauthorized residents—are not considered qualified aliens.) Such eligibility restrictions are not universal, however; all noncitizens, for example, may receive emergency Medicaid benefits.

Because U.S.–born children of noncitizens are themselves citizens, and thus may be eligible for federal benefits not available to their parents, their participation in various programs also affects the federal budget. Their status as citizens may entitle them to receive benefits through Medicaid, SNAP, SSI, and other such programs. In the future, as those citizen-children age and enter the labor force, they will be liable for taxes and ultimately eligible

13. Limits on noncitizens' eligibility to receive some federal benefits were established in title IV of the Personal Responsibility and Work Opportunity Reconciliation Act of 1996, P.L. 104-193, 110 Stat. 2260.

for Social Security and Medicare benefits on their own behalf.

This section provides an overview of the federal benefit programs that would most likely be affected by changes to immigration policy. In addition, it explores how such policy changes would affect federal tax revenues.

The budgetary effects of changes to immigration policy would vary over time. Many of the federal programs discussed in this report limit eligibility or require waiting periods before noncitizens are eligible to receive benefits (see Table 1 on page 3). Future immigration policies that raised immigration rates or changed the immigration status of current noncitizen residents, but left those waiting periods unchanged, would probably have relatively small effects on federal spending over the first five years (the current waiting period for several programs). Thereafter, changes to immigration policy would have larger effects, as more residents became eligible for some programs (such as Medicaid) or grew older and qualified for other programs (such as Social Security and Medicare). However, spending might not change in proportion to the number of people granted eligibility because noncitizens tend to have lower income than citizens and, for a variety of reasons, some people choose not to claim benefits for which they are eligible.

Federal Benefits

Changes to immigration policy could have wide-ranging effects on major federal benefit programs: health care programs for low-income people, SNAP, Social Security, SSI, Medicare, Pell grants, federal student loans, and unemployment insurance. Absent changes in eligibility requirements, the largest costs to the federal government, especially in the first decade, would probably result from additional spending for health care.

In general, noncitizens who might be eligible for many of the major federal spending programs have slightly lower participation rates in those programs than do citizens.[14] It is unclear from the available data, however, whether differences in participation rates were attributable to differences in eligibility, the degree to which eligible

people participate in a benefit program, or some combination of the two.[15]

Health Care Programs for Low-Income People. Health care programs for people with low income include Medicaid, CHIP, and the health insurance subsidies (including premium and cost-sharing assistance) that became available through exchanges beginning in 2014 under the Affordable Care Act. Noncitizens' eligibility for Medicaid and CHIP benefits is limited, but most lawfully present noncitizens can receive insurance subsidies if they meet the qualifications set in the ACA.

Medicaid and CHIP. Medicaid and CHIP are joint federal-state programs that pay for health care services for a variety of low-income people. Most children and pregnant women in low-income families can qualify for Medicaid or CHIP if they are citizens. In addition, some parents of those children also qualify for Medicaid, although the income thresholds vary by state.[16] As a result of the ACA, some nonelderly people with income below 138 percent of the FPL have become eligible for Medicaid starting in 2014.[17] Those new beneficiaries consist primarily of nonelderly adults with low income who are not parents of dependent children.

Medicaid coverage for noncitizens who are not qualified aliens is limited to emergency services; that limitation also applies in most cases during the first five years after an individual becomes a qualified alien. In 2010, about 1.7 million people received such emergency Medicaid benefits at an average cost to the federal government of about $1,100 per person. Under CHIP, states have the option to provide coverage for prenatal care, labor and

---

14. See Leighton Ku and Brian Bruen, *Poor Immigrants Use Public Benefits at a Lower Rate Than Poor Native-Born Citizens*, Economic Development Bulletin 17 (Cato Institute, Center for Global Liberty and Prosperity, March 4, 2013), http://tinyurl.com/bfpbsmn.

15. See, for example, Randolph Capps and others, *The Health and Well-Being of Young Children of Immigrants* (Urban Institute, February 8, 2005), www.urban.org/publications/311139.html; and Michael E. Fix and Jeffrey S. Passel, *Trends in Noncitizens' and Citizens' Use of Public Benefits Following Welfare Reform, 1994–97* (Urban Institute, March 1999), www.urban.org/publications/408086.html.

16. See Congressional Budget Office, *The 2014 Long-Term Budget Outlook* (July 2014), pp. 29–31, www.cbo.gov/publication/45471.

17. The ACA gives states the option to expand eligibility for Medicaid to nonelderly residents with income up to 133 percent of the federal poverty level, commonly referred to as the FPL, which currently is $23,850 for a family of four. The act defines the income used to determine eligibility in a way that effectively increases that threshold to 138 percent of the FPL.

delivery, and postpartum care to low-income women regardless of their immigration status. As of January 2013, 15 states had opted to do so.

In addition, since 2009, states have had the option to use federal matching funds to provide coverage through Medicaid, CHIP, or both to children and to pregnant women during the first five years after they become a qualified alien. As of January 2013, 25 states and the District of Columbia had exercised that option.

After any person has been a qualified alien for five years, states have the option of providing full Medicaid and CHIP benefits if the person meets the other eligibility criteria for the program—and all states have chosen to do so.[18]

Health Insurance Subsidies. The ACA established health insurance exchanges through which certain individuals and families may be eligible for tax credits for premium assistance and reduced cost sharing. For some people, those subsidies substantially reduce the cost of purchasing health insurance. Most people who are in the country legally but lack access to certain other sources of coverage—including Medicaid, CHIP, and affordable employment-based insurance—are eligible for those subsidies if they meet income and certain other requirements. To be eligible for premium assistance credits, a household has to have income between 100 percent and 400 percent of the FPL, and the amount of the credit depends on the cost of the health insurance plan and the person's income. Further, people who are lawfully present and whose income is less than 100 percent of the FPL, but who are ineligible for Medicaid because of their immigration status, are eligible for exchange subsidies as long as they meet other eligibility requirements.[19] Unauthorized residents are not eligible to receive health insurance subsidies.

Supplemental Nutrition Assistance Program. SNAP provides benefits to help people in low-income households purchase food. Eligibility for SNAP is generally based on the income and assets of members of the household or on the participation of household members in other assistance programs.[20]

Unauthorized residents and temporary residents are not eligible for benefits. For LPRs and refugees to qualify, they must meet specific requirements in addition to the usual eligibility criteria. For example, most adult LPRs must wait five years, whereas LPRs under the age of 18 can receive benefits at any point. (Some noncitizens, such as refugees and those granted asylum, are eligible for benefits without a waiting period.)

Social Security. The federal government's largest program in terms of spending, Social Security provides benefits to retired workers (through Old-Age and Survivors Insurance), to people with disabilities (through Disability Insurance, or DI), and to their families, as well as to some survivors of deceased workers. Those benefits are financed primarily by payroll taxes collected on people's earnings. To qualify for retirement benefits, workers must meet a "quarters of coverage" criterion that essentially requires them to have worked in the United States for one-fourth (40 quarters) of their adult life. For younger people with disabilities, fewer quarters are required.[21]

The Social Security program does not impose a citizenship requirement; for example, noncitizens such as LPRs and refugees who meet the program's qualifications may receive benefits.[22] However, Social Security benefits may not be paid to people who are not lawfully present in the United States or who do not live in a specific group of foreign countries in which they may receive benefits.[23]

Supplemental Security Income. SSI provides cash benefits to people with low income and few assets who are dis-

---

18. See, for example, Karina Fortuny and Ajay Chaudry, *A Comprehensive Review of Immigrant Access to Health and Human Services* (Urban Institute, June 2011), www.urban.org/publications/412425.html.

19. See 26 U.S.C. §36B (c)(1)(B) (2012).

20. See Congressional Budget Office, *The Supplemental Nutrition Assistance Program* (April 2012), www.cbo.gov/publication/43173. Additionally, eligible children can receive nutrition assistance through various child nutrition programs—including the National School Lunch Program and the School Breakfast Program, among others—regardless of their legal status. Thus, any change in the total number of children in the country would affect spending for those programs.

21. See Congressional Budget Office, *The 2014 Long-Term Budget Outlook* (July 2014), Chapter 3, www.cbo.gov/publication/45471, and *Social Security Disability Insurance: Participation Trends and Their Fiscal Implications* (July 2010), www.cbo.gov/publication/21638.

22. Section 402 of the Personal Responsibility and Work Opportunity Reconciliation Act of 1996, P.L. 104-193, 8 U.S.C. § 1611(a) (2012).

23. See Social Security Administration, *Social Security: Your Payments While You Are Outside the United States* (September 2013), http://go.usa.gov/BaXJ.

abled, elderly (age 65 or over), or both. The program uses the same medical criteria for adults as those used for DI benefits. All states provide Medicaid coverage for SSI beneficiaries, but some states have more restrictive eligibility requirements than others.[24]

Aside from refugees, people who have been granted asylum, and certain others admitted on humanitarian grounds, noncitizens who entered the United States after 1996 must naturalize or obtain 40 quarters (10 years) of work credit and spend five years as lawful permanent residents to become eligible for the SSI program. In the case of their noncitizen children, eligibility is based on the parents' quarters of work credit. Thus, obtaining SSI benefits is more difficult than qualifying for DI benefits. (DI has less stringent quarters-of-coverage requirements and only requires that the recipient be lawfully present in the country.) Unauthorized residents cannot receive SSI benefits under any circumstances.

Medicare. The Medicare program provides subsidized medical insurance to the elderly and to some people with disabilities. People generally become eligible for Medicare at age 65 (if they have worked long enough to qualify for Social Security retirement benefits) or two years after they qualify for Social Security DI benefits.

As with the Social Security program, Medicare does not impose a citizenship requirement: LPRs, refugees, and people who have been granted asylum may receive benefits if they meet the program's qualifications. Lawfully present noncitizens who do not meet the program's work requirements but who have been LPRs for at least five years can enroll in both Medicare Parts A (Hospital Insurance) and B (Medical Insurance) but must pay premiums to receive benefits. They may also enroll in Part D (prescription drug coverage) if they have also enrolled in both Parts A and B.

People who are not lawfully present in the United States are ineligible to receive Medicare benefits. In addition, Medicare does not provide coverage outside of the United States. Thus, people who work in the United States and pay Medicare taxes but relocate to another country when they are eligible for Medicare benefits do not receive coverage.

Pell Grants and Federal Student Loans. The federal government operates a number of different programs to help students pay for tuition, books, and living expenses at postsecondary institutions. To qualify for federal student aid, such as Pell grants or federal student loans, students who are noncitizens must meet several requirements. In terms of status, they must be one of the following: an LPR; a conditional permanent resident (a noncitizen who gains entrance to the United States because he or she has married a U.S. citizen or an LPR, or has invested in a U.S. business); a refugee; an individual who has been granted asylum; or someone who falls in one of certain other eligible categories of noncitizens.[25] In addition, they must be enrolled in or accepted for enrollment as a regular student in an eligible degree or certificate program; and for Pell grants and subsidized student loans, they must demonstrate financial need.[26] Unlike most other federal benefit programs, it is not necessary to wait at least five years to qualify for Pell grants and federal student loans.

Unemployment Insurance. The unemployment insurance program provides benefits to workers who have become unemployed through no fault of their own and who meet specified criteria. A number of factors determine whether an individual is eligible for unemployment insurance. For example, to qualify for minimum benefits, the worker must have sufficient work history (as specified by state law) in an occupation covered by the Federal Unemployment Tax Act. In addition, an individual who files for benefits must be actively seeking work. As a result, only a fraction of unemployed people collect unemployment benefits.[27]

Noncitizens who work in the country with legal authorization—including LPRs and some temporary workers—are eligible for unemployment insurance benefits if they meet established criteria when they become unem-

24. See Congressional Budget Office, *Supplemental Security Income: An Overview* (December 2012), www.cbo.gov/publication/43759.

25. See Department of Education, "Completing the Free Application for Federal Student Aid (FAFSA), 2013–14" (updated February 5, 2013), http://go.usa.gov/Bx2W.

26. See Congressional Budget Office, *The Pell Grant Program: Recent Growth and Policy Options* (September 2013), www.cbo.gov/publication/44448, and *Costs and Policy Options for Federal Student Loan Programs* (March 2010), www.cbo.gov/publication/21018.

27. See Congressional Budget Office, *Unemployment Insurance in the Wake of the Recent Recession* (November 2012), www.cbo.gov/publication/43734.

ployed.[28] Additional rules specify that the noncitizen worker must still be eligible to work in the United States when he or she receives benefits. Unauthorized workers—including those who are unlawfully present and those who are lawfully present but not authorized to work in the United States—are ineligible for unemployment insurance benefits.[29]

Refundable Tax Credits. Depending on circumstances and an individual's income, the Internal Revenue Service (IRS) may make a payment, in the form of a refundable tax credit, to a person that exceeds his or her tax liability.[30] In addition to the tax credits for health insurance premiums mentioned above, other examples include the earned income tax credit (EITC) and the child tax credit.

To receive a refundable tax credit, an individual generally must file his or her tax return with the IRS, have either a Social Security number or an individual taxpayer identification number (ITIN), and meet various other requirements, depending on the specific credit. Of the existing credits, the EITC has the most stringent requirement for noncitizens. To receive the EITC, the recipient, his or her spouse, and the child or children generally must have a Social Security number that is valid for employment in the United States.[31] Those requirements make it difficult for unauthorized residents to receive the EITC. Criteria for receiving the child tax credit are less strict than those for the EITC, but the child must be a citizen or resident of the United States, and both the child and

---

the filer must have a Social Security number or an ITIN.[32]

Tax Liability

Noncitizens who live and work in the United States are liable for some taxes, and changes in their status or changes in the flow of people entering and leaving the country would affect federal revenues as well as outlays. The extent to which revenues increased or decreased would vary depending on the specifics of the legislation and on the type of tax.

All taxpayers whose income exceeds a certain threshold are required to file a tax return and, if their income is greater than a second threshold, they must pay individual income taxes. If they are employed, income taxes on their earnings are withheld during the year by their employer. Social insurance, or payroll, taxes are also withheld from earnings by employers in full each pay period. Self-employed people generally pay estimated taxes (including both income and social insurance taxes) quarterly. Other federal taxes for which noncitizens may be responsible include excise taxes, estate taxes, and gift taxes.

Changes in federal revenues resulting from changes in immigration policy would depend on whether the policy altered the legal status and number of new or existing residents. If the flow of noncitizens into the country increased, for example, federal revenues would rise when those individuals began to work and pay taxes. If a policy modified the immigration status of unauthorized residents currently living in the country, federal tax revenues also might increase, but the effect on revenues would depend on the way the policy was structured, the extent to which those workers currently pay taxes, and whether the change in their status led to an increase in their

---

28. In contrast with temporary *workers*, temporary *residents* whose authorization to be in the United States depends on employment are not necessarily eligible for unemployment compensation.

29. National Employment Law Project, "Immigrants' Eligibility for Unemployment Compensation" (April 2002), http://tinyurl.com/d6otr2a.

30. For more information about refundable tax credits, see Congressional Budget Office, *Refundable Tax Credits* (January 2013), www.cbo.gov/publication/43767.

31. Taxpayers cannot claim the EITC if the following conditions exist: their Social Security card states "Not Valid for Employment" and their Social Security number was issued specifically so that the taxpayer (and his or her spouse and qualifying children) could get a federally funded benefit, such as Medicaid. See Internal Revenue Service, "Earned Income Credit (EIC)," Publication 596 (December 2014), http://go.usa.gov/Ba5e.

32. The IRS issues ITINs to people who are required to have such identification for tax purposes but are not eligible to obtain a Social Security number because they are not authorized to work. According to a recent report by the Congressional Research Service, it is unclear how many individuals who file taxes with ITINs were unauthorized residents or part of mixed-status families that include both citizens and unauthorized residents. See Congressional Research Service, *Ability of Unauthorized Aliens to Claim Refundable Tax Credits* (July 2012). In January 2013, the IRS tightened the documentation requirements for obtaining an ITIN.

earnings.[33] Two studies have estimated that at least half of unauthorized residents already pay income and payroll taxes.[34]

Proposals That Would Change Noncitizens' Status

Over the past decade, the Congress has considered a variety of proposals that would change the number, type, and legal status of noncitizens in the United States. Certain proposals would modify the visa system for permanent residents and temporary workers and grant legal residency to some or most of the residents currently in the country without authorization. The proposed changes vary greatly in scope and could affect many federal programs and thus have significant effects on the federal budget. Although this report focuses largely on the spending side of the federal budget, changes to immigration policies also could have a significant effect on tax revenues. Some of those proposals would result in net budgetary savings whereas others would result in net budgetary costs.

This report does not address in detail how a change in immigration policy might affect federal spending or tax revenues through its effects on the broader economy—as evidenced in changes to gross domestic product, employment, and total wages. In some instances, when those effects would probably be significant, CBO and JCT have relaxed the long-standing convention of not

incorporating such macroeconomic effects in cost estimates (see Box 2).[35] Immigration legislation also could have a broader set of effects on output and income that have not been reflected in cost estimates. Those additional economic effects include changes in the productivity of labor and capital, the income earned by capital, the rate of return on capital (and therefore the interest rate on government debt), and the differences in wages for workers with different skills. Those effects and their estimated consequences for the federal budget have, on occasion, been discussed in separate reports regarding the proposed legislation.[36]

Earlier this month, the House of Representatives adopted a rule that requires CBO and JCT to include the budgetary feedback of any macroeconomic effects in cost estimates for some major pieces of legislation.[37] Legislation that would make significant changes in immigration policy might be covered by this rule; if so, future cost estimates provided to the House for such legislation will, to the extent practicable, incorporate the sorts of effects described here.

33. According to a study of the effects on the wages of workers who gained legal status as a result of the 1986 Immigration Reform and Control Act, "The postlegalization changes in wage determinants for legalized workers are consistent with labor market mobility, which provides workers with an opportunity to move into jobs that reward existing human capital." See Sherrie A. Kossoudji and Deborah A. Cobb-Clark, "Coming Out of the Shadows: Learning About Legal Status and Wages From the Legalized Population," *Journal of Labor Economics*, vol. 20, no. 3 (July 2002), p. 618, http://tinyurl.com/kaqesty; and Congressional Budget Office, *The Economic Impact of S. 744, the Border Security, Economic Opportunity, and Immigration Modernization Act* (June 2013), www.cbo.gov/publication/44346.

34. See *Economic Report of the President, 2005* (February 2005), Chapter 4, p. 107, http://tinyurl.com/c9kdark; Social Security Administration, Office of the Chief Actuary, "Letter to Senator Richard J. Durbin" (June 5, 2007). Also see Alice H. Wade and others, "Projections of Immigration for the 2008 Social Security Trustees Report," Actuarial Note 148 (Social Security Administration, Office of the Chief Actuary, March 2009), http://go.usa.gov/BaRG.

35. See Congressional Budget Office, letter to the Honorable Patrick J. Leahy providing an estimate for S. 744, the Border Security, Economic Opportunity, and Immigration Modernization Act, as passed by the Senate on June 27, 2013 (July 3, 2013), www.cbo.gov/publication/44397; cost estimate for S. 744, the Border Security, Economic Opportunity, and Immigration Modernization Act (June 18, 2013), http://www.cbo.gov/publication/44225; and letter to the Honorable Paul Ryan describing how CBO would analyze the economic effects of proposals to make major changes in economic policy (May 2, 2013), www.cbo.gov/publication/44109. In addition, see Congressional Budget Office, cost estimate for S. 2611, the Comprehensive Immigration Reform Act of 2006, and *Additional Information on the Estimated Budgetary and Economic Effects of S. 2611* (attachments to a letter to the Honorable Charles E. Grassley, May 16, 2006), www.cbo.gov/publication/17779.

36. See, for example, Congressional Budget Office, *The Economic Impact of S. 744, the Border Security, Economic Opportunity, and Immigration Modernization Act* (June 2013), www.cbo.gov/publication/44346, and *Additional Information on the Estimated Budgetary and Economic Effects of S. 2611* (attachment to a letter to the Honorable Charles E. Grassley, May 16, 2006), www.cbo.gov/publication/17779.

37. See section 2(c) of H. Res. 5, adopted on January 6, 2015, which added clause 8 to Rule XIII. The rule defines major legislation to include bills that would have a gross budgetary effect (before incorporating macroeconomic effects) in a fiscal year equal to or greater than 0.25 percent of GDP—or legislation so designated by certain committee chairmen. However, the rule does not apply to appropriation bills.

Changing the Criteria for Admitting Lawful Permanent Residents

To enter the United States as an LPR or as a temporary resident, a person must obtain a visa from the Department of State and the Department of Homeland Security. To qualify for permanent admission (that is, as an LPR), a foreign-born person must be one of the following: an immediate relative of a U.S. citizen; eligible for family-sponsored preferences; eligible for employment-based preferences; the holder of a diversity program visa; a refugee or a person granted asylum; or someone who meets certain other criteria. According to data from the State Department, the United States granted LPR status to about 1.0 million people in 2013. The wait time varies significantly for both family-sponsored and employment visas. For most categories of family-sponsored visas, the wait time is more than half a decade and for some people it can be more than two decades. For most employment visas, the current wait time is one year or less, although for skilled or professional workers from China and India, the wait time can be almost 10 years or more.[38]

Policies that broadly affected the characteristics of new LPRs—for instance, by shifting permanent visas from a family-based system to a merit-based system that gave priority to workers with particular skills—could have a significant impact on the average educational attainment of LPRs and, as a result, on their average income, earnings, tax payments, and use of federal programs. The Border Security, Economic Opportunity, and Immigration Modernization Act, for example, would establish a point system to determine which applicants received a visa.[39] Alternatively, an independent commission could assess demand from employers each year and determine the number and type of work visas to allocate.[40]

Factors CBO Considers When Estimating the Budgetary Effects of Legislation. The current visa system could be modified in a number of ways. How the policy changed the number and characteristics of people eligible to become LPRs would have implications for federal spending and revenues. Among the issues CBO would consider when estimating the effects of such policy proposals are the following:

■ Would the total number of people entering the country with a visa increase, decrease, or remain roughly unchanged?

■ Would the visa system shift from its current emphasis on family-based immigration to a system that favored skill- or employment-based immigration?

■ How would limits on types of visas be determined, and how often would those limits change?

■ What percentage of potential LPRs would be new entrants, and what percentage would already be in the country and adjusting status?

Effects on Federal Spending and Revenues. Changes to the existing visa system for permanent residents could have significant effects on the U.S. economy and on the federal budget. The direction and magnitude of those effects would depend on whether the policies increased or decreased the total number of LPRs and how the policies affected the demographic makeup of that population. Under current law, permanent residents who meet program requirements are generally eligible to receive benefits after a specified waiting period or period of employment; thus, an increase in the number of LPRs would ultimately increase spending for programs such as Social Security and Medicare. Whether those residents qualify for certain means-tested benefits (such as those provided by Medicaid and SNAP) is determined, in part, by their income.

---

38. There are separate wait times for certain countries such as China, India, Mexico, and the Philippines. See http://travel.state.gov/visa/bulletin/bulletin_1360.html.

39. S. 744, 113th Congress (2013). That point system included various criteria such as employment history, education, the ability to speak English, knowledge of civics, and extended family considerations. Until the available visas were exhausted, visas would be awarded to those applicants with the highest scores. Changes in the skill mix of new LPRs could have other effects on the labor force, including raising productivity among other workers; see Congressional Budget Office, *The Economic Impact of S. 744, the Border Security, Economic Opportunity, and Immigration Modernization Act* (June 2013), www.cbo.gov/publication/44346.

40. For an example of a proposal for such a commission, see Demetrios G. Papademetriou and others, "Harnessing the Advantages of Immigration for a 21st-Century Economy: A Standing Commission on Labor Markets, Economic Competitiveness, and Immigration" (Immigration Policy Institute, May 2009), http://tinyurl.com/2e7q2vw.

Box 2.

Macroeconomic Effects of Changes in Immigration Policy

Following the long-standing convention of not incorporating macroeconomic effects in cost estimates—a practice that has been followed in the Congressional budget process since it was established in 1974—cost estimates produced by the Congressional Budget Office (CBO) and by the staff of the Joint Committee on Taxation (JCT) typically reflect the assumption that macroeconomic variables such as gross domestic product (GDP) and employment remain fixed at the values they are projected to reach under current law. Thus, when estimating the potential effects of legislative proposals on the federal budget, CBO and JCT generally assume that before-tax wages, the labor supply, and other characteristics of the overall economy would not change as a result of the legislation. (In most cases, those effects would be negligible.) This convention has been followed in estimating the costs of legislation that would make small changes to immigration policy.

A change in immigration policy that substantially increased the total population of the United States, however, would cause significant changes in the labor force that were a direct consequence and fundamental objective of the legislation. The magnitude of those changes would depend on the net change in immigration under the policy, as well as how such factors as labor force participation, unemployment rates, average hours of work, and average wages would differ under the policy in comparison with CBO's baseline projections.[1]

In such cases, CBO and JCT have relaxed the standard assumption of not accounting for macroeconomic effects of legislation. An example is the cost estimate for S. 744, the Border Security, Economic Opportunity, and Immigration Modernization Act, as reported by the Senate Judiciary Committee in June 2013. That bill would have significantly increased the size of the U.S. labor force: Relative to CBO's projections under then-current law, enacting that version of S. 744 would have increased the size of the labor force by about 6 million (about 3.5 percent) in 2023 and by about 9 million (about 5 percent) in 2033, CBO and JCT estimated. Employment would have been expected to increase as the labor force expanded because many of the additional immigrants would seek jobs and the larger population would boost demand for goods and services and, in turn, the demand for labor.

---

1. CBO's baseline projections are not intended to be a prediction of future budgetary outcomes; rather, they serve as a neutral benchmark that lawmakers can use to measure the potential effects of tax and spending proposals.

Continued

If the policy change resulted in more LPRs with sufficiently low income to qualify for benefits, costs for those federal programs also would increase. In the first five years, the biggest effect on spending would probably involve the health insurance subsidies established by the ACA; after that, changes in spending for other programs would have increased importance. Tax revenues also would change if the visa system was altered, although whether revenues increased or decreased would depend on the details of the policy. Proposals that changed existing criteria for issuing visas or created new categories of visas tailored to specific groups of people, but that did not change the overall number or characteristics of new LPRs, would probably have little effect on federal programs.

Health Care Programs for Low-Income People, SNAP, and SSI. Proposals that increased the number of permanent residents eligible for benefits from means-tested programs, such as Medicaid, CHIP, subsidies for health insurance obtained through exchanges, SNAP, and SSI, would increase federal expenditures on those programs. Under the programs' current requirements, most people would be subject to a waiting period before receiving benefits. (The exchange subsidies do not require a waiting period, however.) Conversely, changes to the visa system that reduced the number of eligible beneficiaries would result in lower expenditures than are projected under current law.

Box 2.   Continued

Macroeconomic Effects of Changes in Immigration Policy

But following the standard convention of assuming that employment would remain unchanged relative to current law would have implied that any employment of the additional immigrants would be offset one-for-one by lower employment elsewhere in the population. Because that outcome would be highly implausible, CBO and JCT relaxed the assumption of fixed GDP and employment and incorporated into the cost estimate their projections of the legislation's direct effects on the U.S. population, employment, and taxable compensation, which primarily affected the amount of additional tax revenues that would have resulted from enacting the bill.

Nevertheless, to remain as consistent as possible with the estimating rules that CBO and JCT follow for almost all other legislation, the cost estimate for S. 744 did not incorporate the budgetary impact of every economic consequence of the bill. Rather, in a separate report that accompanied the cost estimate, CBO described the effects that were not taken into account in that estimate (specifically, changes in the productivity of labor and capital, the income earned by capital, the rate of return on capital—and therefore the interest rate on government debt and the differences in wages for workers with different skills)

and the additional budgetary effects that would ensue.[2]

CBO and JCT have anticipated taking a similar approach for any future legislation that would make major changes in immigration policy—reflecting any significant changes in the size of the U.S. population and labor force in the cost estimate for the bill and describing any broader macroeconomic effects in supplemental material. However, earlier this month, the House of Representatives adopted a rule that requires CBO and JCT to include the budgetary feedback of any macroeconomic effects in cost estimates for some major pieces of legislation.[3] Legislation that would make significant changes in immigration policy might be covered by this rule; if so, future cost estimates provided to the House for such legislation will, to the extent practicable, incorporate *both* the direct effects of changes in the size of the U.S. population and labor force under the bill *and* any broader macroeconomic effects of the bill.

---

2. See Congressional Budget Office, *The Economic Impact of S. 744, the Border Security, Economic Opportunity, and Immigration Modernization Act* (June 2013), www.cbo.gov/publication/44346.

3. See section 2(c) of H. Res. 5, adopted on January 6, 2015, which added clause 8 to Rule XIII.

Social Security and Medicare. Proposals that increased the number of LPRs would result in greater federal spending for Social Security and Medicare. In the short term, few of those LPRs would qualify for Social Security and Medicare on the basis of age or disability (although, under current law, people can qualify for Social Security disability benefits—and consequently Medicare—and for Social Security survivors' benefits with fewer than 10 years of covered employment). In the long term, federal spending would increase significantly as those people got older and were more susceptible to a disability or reached their retirement age. A reduction in the number of LPRs would have the opposite effect.

Pell Grants and Federal Student Loans. LPRs can qualify for Pell grants and student loans if they meet the standard eligibility criteria that apply to all recipients. Policies that

increased the number of permanent residents would probably result in greater federal spending on those grants and an increase in the volume of student loans.

Unemployment Insurance. Under current law, LPRs qualify for unemployment insurance if they meet the regular eligibility rules. A policy that increased the number of permanent residents would result in a larger workforce. Hence, the number of unemployed at a given unemployment rate would be greater and expenditures for unemployment insurance would be higher.

Refundable Tax Credits, Income Taxes, and Payroll Taxes. Aggregate changes in taxes stemming from policies that changed the number of LPRs in the country would depend on how a change to immigration policy altered the demographic makeup of the population and on the direction and magnitude of those effects. A policy that resulted in an increase in the number of permanent residents at all earnings levels would result in higher total revenues and more spending for refundable tax credits, but the net effect would depend on the specific provisions of the legislation. Policies that favored permanent residents with higher income and reduced the number of permanent residents with lower income would increase revenue from federal income and payroll taxes and decrease spending for refundable tax credits. Conversely, changes to the visa system that increased the number of permanent residents with lower earnings and reduced the number with higher earnings would result in lower revenues from income and payroll taxes and greater spending for refundable tax credits.

Changing the Visa System for Temporary Workers

In the past, the Congress has considered proposals that would increase the number and types of temporary workers in the country without instituting changes to other parts of the visa system. Increases in the number of temporary workers could significantly affect the U.S. economy through, for example, changes in gross domestic product, employment, and total wages. However, such increases would have a smaller impact on the federal budget than increases in the number of permanent residents because temporary workers (like other temporary residents and visitors) generally are ineligible to receive most benefits.

Under current law, temporary visas are available for high-skilled and low-skilled workers. According to data from the State Department, the United States issued about 670,000 temporary visas to temporary workers and their families in 2013.[41]

Many people who are admitted to the United States as temporary workers enter with what is called an H-1B visa. H-1B visas are awarded to workers with "distinguished merit and ability performing services other than a registered nurse." About 153,000 visas of this type were issued in 2013, up from about 111,000 in 2009. Because workers with H-1B visas typically have higher earnings than other foreign-born workers, policies that increased the number of H-1B workers in the country would probably have little impact on federal spending in the short

term but would increase tax revenues.[42] Policies that increased the number of H-1B workers while decreasing the number of visas for new permanent residents would probably result in reduced spending on need-based programs in the short-term.

Coupled with increased border security and internal enforcement efforts, programs that expanded opportunities for both high-skilled and low-skilled temporary workers could result in a net decrease in the number of unauthorized residents in the country; but the effects of such policy changes would go in both directions. On the one hand, people who might otherwise have entered the country illegally might choose to enter through temporary-worker programs. On the other hand, expanded temporary-worker programs might result in an increase in the number of unauthorized residents if those workers overstayed (that is, remained in the country after their authorization has expired). Increased border security and internal enforcement, however, would result in the removal of some people who overstayed and have the additional effect of reducing the number of other unauthorized residents in the country.

In analyzing changes to the visa system for temporary workers, CBO might anticipate the following:

■ A substantial number of people would apply for an expanded number of temporary-worker visas because of employers' demand for workers who can enter the country legally and because workers from other countries tend to seek higher-paying jobs in the United States;

■ At least within the first few years of a policy's enactment, some workers who applied for such visas would be new entrants who would not otherwise have entered the United States, whereas others would have entered the country without authorization;

---

41. Based on data from the Department of State, Bureau of Consular Affairs, *Report of the Visa Office 2013*, Table XVI(B), http://go.usa.gov/eDJC (PDF, 147 KB).

42. In fiscal year 2012, nearly all H-1B visa holders had at least a bachelor's degree, and their median earnings were $70,000. See Department of Homeland Security, *Characteristics of H-1B Specialty Occupation Workers* (June 2013), http://go.usa.gov/eWaw (PDF, 500 KB). By comparison, CBO reported that in calendar year 2011 median earnings were $31,000 among foreign-born men and $24,000 among foreign-born women; see Congressional Budget Office, *A Description of the Immigrant Population—2013 Update* (attachment to a letter to the Honorable Paul Ryan, May 8, 2013), www.cbo.gov/publication/44134.

- Many of those workers would extend their temporary visas and become LPRs if such options were made available as part of a policy granting more temporary-worker visas; and

- Some of the additional temporary workers would overstay their visas and become unauthorized residents. It is unclear, however, whether the demographic and economic characteristics of those unauthorized residents—and thus their rates of eligibility for various federal programs—would be similar to those of the unauthorized residents currently living in the country.

Factors CBO Considers When Estimating the Budgetary Effects of Legislation. The specific provisions of a new policy would greatly affect the number of people who received temporary-worker visas and, subsequently, the costs of a variety of federal services. Among the issues that CBO would consider when estimating the effects of such policy proposals are the following:

- Would family members of temporary workers be eligible for similar residency status?

- Would people be required to leave the country for some portion of the year?

- How much would it cost (in the form of fines or fees) to participate in the program?

- Would new types of visas or expanded numbers of visas for temporary workers be tied directly to those workers' employers?

- Would temporary workers ultimately be eligible for LPR status, citizenship, or some other long-term-resident status?

- What would the time frame be for achieving such status?

- What actions would temporary workers need to take to obtain status as an LPR?

Different combinations of policy changes could significantly affect the types of workers who entered the country. For example, a policy that required workers to pay a substantial fee *and* leave the United States for some period of time would be less onerous for those workers who have the means and capability to incur such costs and therefore are better equipped than other workers to adapt to such a policy.

Effects on Federal Spending and Revenues. Under current law, temporary workers are typically not eligible for many federal programs; thus, the direct impact on the federal budget of increasing the number of visas for temporary workers would probably be small in the short term. However, if legislation both expanded the number of available LPR visas and allowed temporary workers to adjust their status and eventually become citizens, the long-term fiscal impact of those residents and their citizen children could be significant. In addition to spending on program benefits, DHS would incur administrative costs to process visa applications, and SSA would incur costs to provide Social Security numbers and cards to temporary workers. The increased costs for DHS would be at least partially offset by collections from application fees. An increase in the number of temporary workers also might result in an increase in revenues from income and payroll taxes; however, temporary workers' tax liability would depend on the specific category of their visa and the length of time they have been in the country.

Health Care Programs for Low-Income People, SNAP, and SSI. Because of current program restrictions, temporary workers are not eligible for CHIP, SNAP, or SSI but are eligible for emergency Medicaid services if they meet other eligibility requirements for Medicaid. Because they are lawfully present in the United States, temporary workers may also be eligible to receive subsidies for health insurance through the insurance exchanges created by the ACA if they meet income requirements and do not have access to certain other sources of health insurance coverage. (However, if temporary workers are lawfully present in the country for a short time, they may be less likely to apply for and receive subsidies through the exchanges.) Hence, an increase in the number of visas for temporary workers would probably lead to higher federal spending for emergency Medicaid and subsidies for health insurance exchanges. In addition, depending on the economic situation of the household and other factors, children born in the United States to those new entrants might qualify for all five of the programs discussed here.

Social Security and Medicare. Depending on the proposed change to immigration policy, temporary workers might or might not be eligible for these programs. Changes that allowed temporary workers to qualify for such benefits would lead more of them to collect Social Security and Medicare benefits the longer they remained in the country—primarily because, as they aged, their likelihood of disability or retirement would rise. In the case of Social Security, such workers also would be more likely to have earned the necessary quarters of coverage to qualify for benefits. Under current law, most workers who gain LPR or citizenship status following admission as a temporary worker eventually qualify for Medicare.

Pell Grants and Federal Student Loans. Temporary workers are not eligible for federal student loans and grants. Thus, unless changes to the visa program were accompanied by changes in the eligibility requirements for those programs, changes to the number or type of temporary-worker visas would not result in more federal expenditures.

Unemployment Insurance. Temporary workers are generally eligible for unemployment insurance provided they remain legally eligible to work while they are unemployed. An increase in the number of temporary workers would result in a larger workforce. Therefore, the number of unemployed at a given unemployment rate would be greater and expenditures for unemployment insurance would be higher.

Refundable Tax Credits, Income Taxes, and Payroll Taxes. The tax liability of temporary workers in the United States depends on the specific category of their visa and how long they have been in the country. For example, foreign agricultural workers (holders of H-2A visas) are exempt from paying Social Security and Medicare taxes on income earned from agricultural work. Those workers may be responsible for federal income taxes depending on how long they have been in the country, the amount of income they earned in the United States, and other factors. Some temporary workers may be exempt from federal personal income taxes depending on their country of origin. Additionally, some temporary workers may be eligible for refundable tax credits, but that eligibility depends on a number of factors, including the type of work the person is authorized to undertake and the number of days he or she has spent in the United States.[43]

---

43. See Internal Revenue Service, "U.S. Tax Guide for Aliens," Publication 519 (last updated January 13, 2015), www.irs.gov/pub519.

Granting Legal Status to Unauthorized Residents

The Congress has considered several policy options in the past that would confer some type of legal status on some of the roughly 11 million to 12 million noncitizens who live in the United States without authorization. Provisions of proposed legalization have typically included certain general eligibility requirements: For instance, people would have to prove that they have been in the country for a specified number of years or from a certain date, that they have successfully completed a security background check, that they have not been convicted of serious crimes while in the country, and that they have paid certain fines and fees.

In the past, CBO has estimated the budgetary effects of policies that would confer legal status on unauthorized residents in the following categories:

■ People who are unlawfully present and working in the agricultural sector;

■ People who entered the United States without authorization when they were young (for an example of such a proposal, see Box 3 on page 24); and

■ Most other unauthorized residents, regardless of their occupation or age of entry.[44]

Factors CBO Considers When Estimating the Budgetary Effects of Legislation. The specific provisions of legalization policies, if implemented, would greatly affect the number of people who participate in federal programs as well as the costs of providing benefits and related government services. Among the issues CBO would consider when estimating the effects of such policy proposals are the following:

---

44. See, for example, Congressional Budget Office, letter to the Honorable Patrick J. Leahy providing an estimate for S. 744, the Border Security, Economic Opportunity, and Immigration Modernization Act, as passed by the Senate on June 27, 2013 (July 3, 2013), www.cbo.gov/publication/44397; cost estimate for S. 744, the Border Security, Economic Opportunity, and Immigration Modernization Act (June 18, 2013), www.cbo.gov/publication/44225; cost estimate for S. 3992, the Development, Relief, and Education for Alien Minors Act of 2010 (December 2010), www.cbo.gov/publication/21952; cost estimate for Senate Amendment 1150 to S. 1348, the Comprehensive Immigration Reform Act of 2007 (June 4, 2007), www.cbo.gov/publication/18716; and cost estimate for S. 2611, the Comprehensive Immigration Reform Act of 2006 (August 2006), www.cbo.gov/publication/18065.

■ Would the change in legal status be temporary or permanent?

■ If previously unauthorized residents became LPRs, would they be eligible for the same benefits available to other LPRs or would the benefits be restricted?

■ Would people granted legal status be eligible to become U.S. citizens?

■ Would waiting periods for benefits be similar to those that exist under current law?

■ Would spouses and children also be eligible for legal status? If so, would all dependents be eligible or only those who currently live in the country without authorization?

■ How much would eligible people have to pay in fines or fees to participate in the program?

Effects on Federal Spending and Revenues. Whether, and to what extent, newly authorized residents qualified for federal benefits would have significant budgetary implications. Their eligibility for certain benefits would depend in part on whether they were granted temporary authorization or LPR status. Policies that provided currently unauthorized residents with LPR status or otherwise increased the number of residents with LPR status would result in more spending for federal programs. Legalization policies also might result in increased tax revenues, stemming mostly from some additional payment of income and payroll taxes.

Policies that allow currently unauthorized residents to become LPRs would, over time, increase spending for a variety of federal benefits, including those provided by health care programs for low-income people (specifically, Medicaid, CHIP, and subsidies for the purchase of health insurance through the exchanges established by the ACA), SNAP, Social Security, Medicare, and various refundable tax credits. Several other federal programs, such as SSI, Pell grants, and unemployment insurance also could experience spending increases. In accordance with current law, many of these programs already require applicants to demonstrate that they have lived in the country legally for a certain period. However, for the health insurance exchange subsidies, no such residency requirement applies to lawful residents. If the policy changing the status of currently unauthorized residents

did not specifically make them ineligible for the subsidies, much of the budgetary impact in the first few years after enactment of a change in their status would stem from added costs for those subsidies. After that time, changes in spending for other programs would have increased importance.

In addition to increases in spending for benefits, government agencies would incur higher administrative and processing costs. For example, a policy that resulted in an increase in the number of visa applications would add to DHS's administrative costs, and providing newly authorized residents with Social Security numbers and cards would lead to increases in costs for SSA. The additional costs incurred by DHS, however, might be offset by collections from application fees. Finally, proposals that required applicants to pay monetary penalties as well as application fees in order to change their legal status would result in additional revenues.

Health Care Programs for Low-Income People. Policies that conferred legal status on formerly unauthorized residents could result in increased spending for Medicaid, CHIP, and subsidies provided through the health insurance exchanges.

Unauthorized residents who are currently in the country already qualify for emergency Medicaid services if they meet income and other eligibility criteria. To the extent that legalization programs resulted in spouses and children entering the country, some of those new entrants also might qualify for emergency Medicaid services. If LPR status was a component of the legalization process, those LPRs who met income and other eligibility criteria would qualify for all medical services under Medicaid five years after becoming an LPR.

For children who are unauthorized, eligibility for CHIP depends on whether the state in which they live chooses to provide benefits to them. Therefore, policies that increased the number of lawfully present children in the United States could ultimately lead to higher enrollment in CHIP and could lead to greater federal spending for the program, assuming that sufficient funds were made available for the program. Many would have to wait five years to obtain full coverage.

Similarly, policies that increased the number of lawfully present people would result in more people qualifying for exchange subsidies; unless otherwise specified, they

Box 3.

Estimating the Effects of the DREAM Act on the Federal Budget

Previous estimates of proposed legislation that would change federal immigration policies related to young people illustrate how the Congressional Budget Office (CBO) projects the cost of such policies to the federal government. For example, in December 2010, CBO and the staff of the Joint Committee on Taxation (JCT) prepared cost estimates for two versions of the Development, Relief, and Education of Alien Minors Act of 2010 (DREAM Act). Both bills (S. 3992 and H.R. 6497) would have provided conditional nonimmigrant status for unauthorized residents who met specific requirements:

■ They were less than 16 years of age when they entered the country;

■ They had lived in the United States for at least five years before the bill's enactment;

■ They had graduated from high school, obtained a GED certificate, or were high school students who had been admitted to an institution of higher education; and

■ They had completed background checks and paid any federal taxes due.

For the most part, the bills' eligibility requirements for conditional nonimmigrant status were similar, although the length of legal status and the fees charged for participation differed. The Senate bill would have provided conditional nonimmigrant status for 10 years. After 10 years, residents would be eligible for lawful permanent resident (LPR) status if they had received a college degree or served at least two years in the military. The version of the legislation introduced in the House of Representatives would have provided conditional nonimmigrant status for an initial period of five years. That status could have been extended for an additional five years if the individual had earned a degree, completed at least two years toward a bachelor's (or higher) degree, or served at least two years in the military. After the five-year extension, the resident would be eligible for LPR status.

When these proposals were being considered, CBO estimated that, by 2020, fewer residents would have been granted conditional nonimmigrant status under the provisions of the House bill (700,000 residents) than under the Senate proposal (1.1 million residents). Those differences reflect, among other factors, the likelihood that many people who would have obtained the initial five-year status in the House version would not have met the requirements for the extension.

Continued

---

would be eligible for those subsidies without a waiting period. Because unauthorized workers tend to have lower incomes than other groups, many would probably have income low enough to qualify for generous exchange subsidies, if they lacked access to certain other sources of coverage (including Medicaid, CHIP, and affordable employment-based insurance) and met certain other requirements.

SNAP. If LPR status was a component of the legalization process, granting that status to children under the age of 18 would result in their immediately qualifying for SNAP benefits as long as they met the program's other eligibility requirements. If a policy was adopted that conferred LPR status on unauthorized residents over the age of 18 but maintained current eligibility rules—specifically, the five-year waiting period—those workers

Box 3.   **Continued**

Estimating the Effects of the DREAM Act on the Federal Budget

The estimates of changes in federal revenues and spending depended on how many people CBO anticipated would attain conditional nonimmigrant status and subsequently become LPRs. By granting conditional nonimmigrant status to some previously unauthorized residents, both bills would have increased the number of authorized workers, thereby resulting in more revenues from individual and corporate income taxes and from social insurance taxes. On balance, JCT estimated that the Senate bill would have increased federal revenues by $2.3 billion over 10 years, whereas the House bill, which affected fewer people, would have boosted revenues by $1.7 billion over 10 years.

Both bills would have also resulted in changes in direct spending for refundable tax credits, Social Security, Medicare, Pell grants, federal student loans, and activities of the Department of Homeland Security. CBO estimated that the Senate version would have increased net direct spending by about $1.1 billion over the 2011–2020 period, whereas the House version would have decreased net direct spending by about $500 million over the same period. (Direct spending is the budget authority provided by laws other than appropriation acts and the outlays that result from that budget authority.) Thus, both bills would have resulted in changes in revenues and direct

spending that would have reduced federal budget deficits in the 10 years following enactment. CBO estimated that, if implemented, both bills would have resulted in the eventual conversion of some conditional nonimmigrants to LPR status after 2020 and would have led to increased spending in subsequent years for subsidies provided through federal health insurance exchanges, Medicaid, and the Supplemental Nutrition Assistance Program.

Both bills would have specifically banned conditional nonimmigrants from participating in health insurance exchanges and receiving premium tax credits under the Affordable Care Act.[1] Absent that specification, CBO would have estimated that both bills would have entailed significant spending by the federal government for those subsidies.

Future estimates for similar legislation would probably differ because of recent administrative changes implemented by the Department of Homeland Security (see Box 1 on page 9).

---

1. As referred to in this report, the Affordable Care Act comprises the Patient Protection and Affordable Care Act (Public Law 111-148) and the health care provisions of the Health Care and Education Reconciliation Act of 2010 (P.L. 111-152), as affected by subsequent judicial decisions, statutory changes, and administrative actions.

---

who met the program's other eligibility requirements could eventually receive SNAP benefits.

Social Security. People who are not lawfully present in the United States are barred from receiving Social Security benefits. Thus, under current law, those individuals may pay Social Security taxes but cannot qualify for retirement, disability, or survivors' benefits. If they are lawfully present, they can receive such benefits once they meet the program's requirements.

Proposals that would grant lawful presence to many unauthorized workers could increase the number of future Social Security beneficiaries. Various sources—data from the Census Bureau's Current Population Survey, research by the Pew Hispanic Center, and studies involving people who obtained legal status under the Immigration Reform and Control Act of 1986—indicate that those workers tend to be younger than the rest of the

U.S. workforce.[45] Because younger workers are less likely to qualify for and claim Social Security benefits than older workers, CBO expects that relatively few of the people directly affected by legalization proposals would qualify for Social Security retirement, disability, or survivors' benefits in the near term, although those numbers would grow in subsequent years. Some proposals could prohibit any unauthorized employment undertaken by such individuals from counting toward their eligibility for Social Security even if they did eventually receive authorization to work. The ability or inability of a formerly unauthorized worker to apply those employment periods to future benefits would affect federal outlays for the program. In addition, depending on the specific provisions of the legislation, people who previously paid Social Security taxes using a stolen or fake Social Security number might be able to claim benefits in the future by using a legitimate Social Security number or by claiming credits earned while using a fraudulent Social Security number.

SSI. Because adults' eligibility for SSI requires five years of lawful permanent residency and a work history spanning 10 years for those who have not naturalized, conferring legal status on currently unauthorized residents would initially affect the SSI program mostly by increasing the rate at which their U.S.–born children received program benefits. (Their foreign-born children also must spend five years as LPRs to receive benefits. Foreign-born children who do not meet that residency requirement would not be eligible for benefits unless their eligibility was specified in the legislation.) Although the U.S.–born children are already citizens by virtue of their birth in the United States, their parents might be more willing to seek benefits for their offspring once they themselves attained legal status.

Medicare. As with Social Security, proposals that would grant lawful presence to unauthorized residents would result in a small increase in the number of Medicare beneficiaries in the near term but have a greater impact in the longer term as those workers aged and then claimed benefits. In addition, depending on the exact nature of the policy change, people who qualified for Social Security Disability Insurance also might be eligible for Medicare after a two-year waiting period.[46] Some people, however, might choose to move back to the country in which they were born (or to some other country outside of the United States) and would therefore no longer qualify for benefits.

Pell Grants and Federal Student Loans. LPRs are eligible to receive federal student aid on the same basis as citizens. Hence, allowing the number of LPRs in the country to grow would probably boost the number of people who apply for such aid. Legalization policies that increased the number of LPRs or conditional permanent residents could boost enrollment at postsecondary institutions as newly eligible students qualified for federal grants and loans.

Unemployment Insurance. Unauthorized workers are not eligible to receive unemployment insurance benefits if they lose a job. An increase in the number of authorized workers would affect outlays for unemployment insurance benefits by increasing the number of people who could be eligible for benefits in the future, assuming they met other eligibility criteria as determined by their state. Because states finance the cost of most unemployment benefits through taxes on employment (both of which are reflected in the federal budget), the net effect on the federal budget from any increase in unemployment benefits that stemmed from changes in immigration would be small.

Refundable Tax Credits. Granting lawful presence and work authorization to unauthorized residents would probably increase the total amount of refundable tax credits provided through the tax system. Relative to native-born citizens and foreign-born residents authorized to be in the United States, a higher proportion of unauthorized workers would be eligible for refundable tax credits because they tend to have lower income than other groups. In addition, once granted legal status, more

---

45. See, for example, Sherrie A. Kossoudji and Deborah A. Cobb-Clark, "Coming Out of the Shadows: Learning About Legal Status and Wages From the Legalized Population," *Journal of Labor Economics*, vol. 20, no. 3 (2002), http://tinyurl.com/kaqesty; and Nancy Rytina, "IRCA Legalization Effects: Lawful Permanent Residence and Naturalization Through 2001" (paper presented at a conference on the Effects of Immigrant Legalization Programs on the United States: Scientific Evidence on Immigrant Adaptation and Impacts on U.S. Economy and Society, National Institutes of Health, October 25, 2002), http://tinyurl.com/ls4vtvx.

46. See Congressional Budget Office, *Policy Options for the Social Security Disability Insurance Program* (July 2012), www.cbo.gov/publication/43421, and *Social Security Disability Insurance: Participation Trends and Their Fiscal Implications* (July 2010), www.cbo.gov/publication/21638.

formerly unauthorized workers would probably earn taxable income instead of receiving informal payments that are not reported to the IRS; that change might make them eligible for such tax credits.

Income and Payroll Taxes. According to one estimate, at least half of unauthorized residents pay income taxes and Social Security taxes through their employer (even though they are not eligible to receive Social Security benefits).[47] If some were granted legal status, the proportion paying income and payroll taxes would probably increase. In addition, more revenues would probably be generated if the policy allowed spouses and children of unauthorized immigrants who were not currently in the United States to enter the country and work.

Proposals Related to Enforcement and Workplace Verification

Proposals to address the enforcement of immigration law generally aim to enhance border security and internal enforcement, and to improve systems and procedures for verifying employees' legal status at the workplace. The budgetary effects of such proposals would depend on the costs of implementing them and on their effectiveness in reducing the number of unauthorized residents; a reduction in the number of unauthorized residents would decrease costs for certain federal programs but also would result in a loss of federal tax receipts. Funding for such proposals could be provided in immigration legislation (which would result in outlays categorized as mandatory spending) or could depend on annual appropriation acts (which would result in outlays categorized as discretionary spending).

Increasing Border Security and Internal Enforcement

Slowing the flow of illegal immigration into the United States and decreasing the employment of unauthorized residents would require the development and implementation of well-designed and well-coordinated programs and processes. The goal of such programs and procedures would be twofold: to make it more difficult for people to enter the country without authorization; and to make it easier for officials to identify, locate, and remove those who entered without authorization or who remained after their authorized stay had ended. Funding for border secu-

rity has risen sharply in recent years, and estimated net flows of unauthorized migrants to the United States have fallen in recent years. However, it is unclear how much of that decrease is attributable to stepped-up enforcement activities and how much is attributable to the downturn in employment associated with the global recession, or to other factors.[48]

Policies That Would Increase Border Security and Internal Enforcement. Policies designed to enhance border security and internal enforcement generally focus on the following four activities: increasing the number of personnel responsible for enforcement, improving border infrastructure and technologies, expanding identification systems, and improving cooperation with state and local governments.

More Personnel. Employing and training additional people to enforce U.S. immigration laws and prosecute violators would require increased federal spending for those purposes. For example, CBO has analyzed several proposals that would have included funding for additional Border Patrol agents (to increase the interdiction of people trying to enter the country illegally) and additional federal judges (to speed up the process of removing people in violation of immigration laws).[49]

Improved Border Infrastructure and Technologies. Improving the kinds and amount of equipment, infrastructure, and technology that are used to secure the country's borders also would necessitate increased federal spending. Such improvements could include, for example, building

---

47. See *Economic Report of the President, 2005* (February 2005), http://tinyurl.com/c9kdark.

48. See, for example, Jeffrey S. Passel, D'Vera Cohn, and Ana Gonzalez-Barrera, *Net Migration From Mexico Falls to Zero— And Perhaps Less* (Pew Hispanic Center, April 23, 2012), http://tinyurl.com/cfcka2j.

49. See, for example, Congressional Budget Office, letter to the Honorable Patrick J. Leahy providing an estimate for S. 744, the Border Security, Economic Opportunity, and Immigration Modernization Act, as passed by the Senate on June 27, 2013 (July 3, 2013), www.cbo.gov/publication/44397; cost estimate for Senate amendment 1150 to S. 1348, the Comprehensive Immigration Reform Act of 2007 (June 4, 2007), www.cbo.gov/publication/18716; cost estimate for S. 2611, the Comprehensive Immigration Reform Act of 2006 (August 18, 2006), www.cbo.gov/publication/18065; cost estimate for H.R. 4437, the Border Protection, Antiterrorism, and Illegal Immigration Control Act of 2005 (December 13, 2005), www.cbo.gov/publication/17549; and cost estimate for H.R. 4312, the Border Security and Terrorism Prevention Act of 2005 (December 6, 2005), www.cbo.gov/publication/17539.

Box 4.

Existing Internal Enforcement Programs

Changes to immigration policy could include new programs and technologies to improve the enforcement of immigration law within the borders of the United States. Two existing enforcement programs could be used as the basis for future policies. In 2002, the Department of Homeland Security (DHS) created the United States Visitor and Immigration Status Indicator Technology program to help identify people who remain in the country after their authorization has expired. Yet, according to the Government Accountability Office, DHS has not implemented the portion of the system that would monitor and confirm when people leave the country.[1]

Secure Communities, which is administered by Immigration and Customs Enforcement (ICE), is another identification program that leverages existing information-sharing capability between DHS and the Department of Justice to identify foreign-born residents who are arrested for committing a crime and taken into custody by local law-enforcement agencies. According to reports issued by ICE, between

October 2008 and August 31, 2014, the Secure Communities program led to the removal of about 375,000 people, 121,000 of whom were charged with or convicted of aggravated felonies. Although the program has proven effective at identifying people potentially eligible for deportation, some observers have expressed concern about its implementation and about its potential effects on relationships between local law-enforcement agencies and the foreign-born residents living in those communities. On November 20, 2014, DHS announced that it would end the Secure Communities program and replace it with the Priority Enforcement Program.[2]

---

1. See testimony of Rebecca Gambler, Director, Homeland Security and Justice, Government Accountability Office, before the Subcommittee on Border and Maritime Security of the House Committee on Homeland Security, *Immigration Enforcement: Preliminary Observations on DHS's Overstay Enforcement Efforts* (May 21, 2013), http://go.usa.gov/BsBH.

2. The Priority Enforcement Program will use biometric data submitted to federal law enforcement databases but will limit the people that ICE transfers to federal custody to those who are convicted of offenses and are a "priority" for enforcement action, including people who pose a threat to national security, border security, and public safety and those who have been convicted of three or more misdemeanors or a single significant misdemeanor. See Jeh Charles Johnson, Secretary, Department of Homeland Security, memorandum about the discontinuation of the Secure Communities program and the establishment of the Priority Enforcement Program (November 20, 2014), http://go.usa.gov/eWCx (PDF, 1.50 MB), and memorandum about policies for the apprehension, detention, and removal of undocumented immigrants (November 20, 2014, http://go.usa.gov/eWrz (PDF, 3 MB).

---

and maintaining border fences, deploying additional mobile, video, and other surveillance systems, and deploying and operating manned and unmanned aerial vehicles.

Expanded Identification Systems. The Pew Hispanic Center has estimated that 40 percent to 50 percent of people who are now residing in the United States without authorization entered the country by legal means.[50] Therefore, a more effective immigration control program could involve additional internal enforcement aimed at

identifying those people, as well as improved border security (see Box 4).

Improved Cooperation With State and Local Governments. To implement immigration-related enforcement activities, the federal government sometimes provides training to state and local law enforcement officers.[51] For example, the Section 287(g) program authorizes the federal government to enter into agreements with state and local law enforcement agencies.[52] Those agreements allow police officers to screen individuals who have been charged with nonimmigration offenses to determine if they are in violation of immigration law. Authorized officers are able to search selected federal databases and conduct interviews to assist in the identification of people living in the

---

50. Pew Hispanic Center, "Modes of Entry for the Unauthorized Migrant Population" (May 22, 2006), http://tinyurl.com/korn9w9.

country illegally. In 2012, DHS announced that it would not renew the 287(g) task force agreements because other programs, such as Secure Communities, were more effective.

Factors CBO Considers When Estimating the Budgetary Effects of Legislation. When assessing the impact of proposed changes to border and internal enforcement policies, CBO would consider the following:

■ To what extent would the policy require new enforcement activities at different points of entry?

■ Would the policy require that additional federal employees be hired and, if so, at what cost?

■ Given the complexities involved in hiring and training immigration law enforcement officials, including high rates of turnover, is it feasible to sustain new, higher staffing levels?

■ Would the policy require the creation of new technology for border surveillance?

■ Does the policy include provisions to identify people who remain in the country after their authorization to do so has expired?

■ To what degree would the policy require the federal government to compensate state and local governments for enforcing immigration law?

■ How effective would the policy be at diminishing the net inflow of unauthorized residents?

51. In recent years, in addition to working with the federal government, many states have enacted their own legislation that addresses unauthorized immigration and other immigration-related policies. The strict immigration requirements enacted in Arizona in 2010 as part of the Support Our Law Enforcement and Safe Neighborhoods Act—which served as a model for legislation in other states—were challenged by the federal government. In June 2012, the Supreme Court ruled in *Arizona v. United States*, 132 S.Ct. 2492, that several provisions were unconstitutional.

52. Sec. 287(g) of the Immigration and Nationality Act, 8 U.S.C. §1357(g) (2012). The program initially consisted of two components, task-force agreements and jail enforcement agreements. The task-force agreements authorized state and local law enforcement officers to identify and arrest some people on federal immigration charges as part of their regular law enforcement duties.

Effects on Federal Spending and Revenues. Implementing such policies would require increased funding, the amount of which would depend on the number of additional federal employees that would be needed and the costs to develop and acquire whatever facilities and equipment would be necessary. In addition, increased border security and other enforcement measures—as well as a mandatory employment verification system to deter the hiring of unauthorized workers (discussed in the next section)—could affect the federal budget by changing the net flow of unauthorized residents into the country. On the one hand, fewer people might enter illegally because crossing the border would be more difficult and remaining in the country would be harder without legal status. On the other hand, tighter border enforcement might encourage people to stay in the United States because it would be harder to get back in. And the enactment of legislation that included provisions conferring legal status on those in the country unlawfully might encourage more people to try to enter the United States illegally (in the hope of benefiting from a future legalization program).

The resulting budgetary effects are difficult to assess. They would depend on a number of factors about which there is little reliable information: the number of illegal border crossings that would occur under current law; the extent to which new enforcement activities would defer, delay, or otherwise modify the behavior of potential unlawful border-crossers; and how administrative and enforcement procedures would change in response to those behaviors.

In the past, CBO has estimated that wide-ranging changes in immigration policy would reduce the net annual flow of unauthorized residents by one-quarter.[53] More recently, CBO estimated that the Border Security, Economic Opportunity, and Immigration Modernization Act, as passed by the Senate in 2013, would reduce the net annual flow of unauthorized residents by between one-third and one-half.[54] The estimated impact of any

53. See Congressional Budget Office, cost estimate for Senate amendment 1150 to S. 1348, the Comprehensive Immigration Reform Act of 2007 (June 2007), www.cbo.gov/publication/18716.

54. See Congressional Budget Office, letter to the Honorable Patrick J. Leahy providing an estimate for S. 744, the Border Security, Economic Opportunity, and Immigration Modernization Act, as passed by the Senate on June 27, 2013 (July 3, 2013), www.cbo.gov/publication/44397.

future legislation on those flows will depend on CBO's judgment of what the net flows of unauthorized migrants would be under current law and an assessment of how the proposed legislation would affect those flows. CBO's earlier estimates of those effects may or may not be applicable to future proposals. Estimated net flows of unauthorized migrants to the United States have fallen to nearly zero or even reversed in recent years—that is, more unauthorized residents may have left the country than have arrived.[55] Those developments are attributable to a variety of factors, including the downturn in employment associated with the global recession and changes in U.S. border security.

Decreases in the net inflows of unauthorized migrants would lead to reduced spending on emergency Medicaid services and child nutrition programs because fewer people would receive benefits. But some unauthorized residents pay payroll and income taxes, so a reduction in their number also might result in a loss of tax revenues.

Improving Verification of People's Eligibility to Work

Some proposals to reduce the number of unauthorized residents in the United States focus on making unlawful presence less attractive by restricting access to employment and increasing the security of identity documents. Under current law, noncitizens must have explicit employment authorization to work in the United States, and employers are not allowed to hire unauthorized workers. However, an estimated 8 million unauthorized residents work in the country.[56] Some employers knowingly hire unauthorized workers whereas others cannot detect fraudulent or fraudulently used documentation.

Under current law, newly hired workers must present two forms of identification to their employers and complete an I-9 form attesting that they are eligible to work in the United States. About two dozen documents can be

accepted as proof of identity; but the issuing agent is not required to verify the legitimacy of those documents. Unauthorized workers can procure fraudulent documents or use authentic documents that were falsely obtained to satisfy the I-9 requirements.

The E-Verify program, administered by DHS, is an online system that employers can use to confirm that newly hired employees are eligible to work. Participation in the system is voluntary for most employers. Federal agencies and contractors, as well as some companies that have been found in violation of hiring laws, are required to use E-verify. In addition, some state and local governments have required employers in their jurisdiction to use the system.[57] As of January 2015, almost 570,000 employers were registered users of the E-Verify program, representing more than 1.8 million hiring sites. In fiscal year 2014, the E-Verify system processed more than 28 million queries.[58]

Factors CBO Considers When Estimating the Budgetary Effects of Proposed Legislation. When estimating the cost of proposals to change work verification systems, CBO would consider the following questions:

- Would the new system be mandatory for all employees or would it apply only to those who are newly hired?

- How many people would need to have their status verified?

- Does the existing E-Verify system have the capacity to confirm the status of all employees or would changes be necessary?

- Would a new system rely on existing identification documents, or would federal agencies be required to supply new ones?

- Would biometric identifiers—which identify people by their physical characteristics or traits, such as fingerprints, handprints, or DNA—be required?

55. See Jeffrey S. Passel, D'Vera Cohn, and Ana Gonzales-Barrera, *Net Migration From Mexico Falls to Zero—And Perhaps Less* (Pew Hispanic Center, April 23, 2012), http://tinyurl.com/cfcka2j; and Jeffrey S. Passel and D'Vera Cohn, *Unauthorized Immigrants: 11.1 Million in 2011* (Pew Hispanic Center, December 6, 2012), http://tinyurl.com/m39g5wp.

56. See Jeffrey S. Passel, D'Vera Cohn, and Molly Rohal, *Unauthorized Immigrant Totals Rise in 7 States, Fall in 14* (Pew Hispanic Center, November 18, 2014), http://tinyurl.com/nf9mwzf (PDF, 2.33 MB).

57. For an analysis of Arizona's requirement for employers to use E-verify, see, for example, Alex Nowrasteh, *The Economic Case Against Arizona's Immigration Laws*, Policy Analysis No. 709 (Cato Institute, September 25, 2012) http://tinyurl.com/l992jks.

58. Data about the Employment Eligibility Verification Program provided to CBO by staff of the Citizenship and Immigration Services.

■ What recourse or compensation would be available to workers who were incorrectly identified as not authorized to work?

Effects on Federal Spending and Revenues. If all employers were required to use the E-Verify system, and if employers needed to confirm the status of all employees, DHS would need additional resources for staff, technological components, and overhead to handle the increased workload. The Social Security Administration also would need additional resources to upgrade technology and hire new employees to resolve issues that arose when E-verify could not confirm that a person was eligible for work.

Expanding the E-Verify system without other changes to current policy would probably result in decreased federal revenues because it would probably lead to an increase in the number of unauthorized workers being paid outside of the tax system. Some employers who currently withhold income and payroll taxes from the wages of unauthorized workers and report those amounts to the IRS through the use of an ITIN or other employee identification number would no longer withhold or report such taxes.

Appendix:
Recent Congressional Budget Office Reports on Immigration and Selected Cost Estimates for Legislation Related to Immigration

Reports

The Economic Impact of S. 744, the Border Security, Economic Opportunity, and Immigration Modernization Act (June 2013), www.cbo.gov/publication/44346.

A Description of the Immigrant Population—2013 Update (attachment to a letter to the Honorable Paul Ryan, May 8, 2013), www.cbo.gov/publication/44134.

Letter to the Honorable Paul Ryan describing how CBO would analyze the economic effects of proposals to make major changes in immigration policy (May 2, 2013), www.cbo.gov/publication/44109.

A Description of the Immigrant Population: An Update (June 2011), www.cbo.gov/publication/41453.

Migrants' Remittances and Related Economic Flows (February 2011), www.cbo.gov/publication/22012.

Immigration Policy in the United States: An Update (December 2010), www.cbo.gov/publication/21921.

The Role of Immigrants in the U.S. Labor Market: An Update (July 2010), www.cbo.gov/publication/21656.

Cost Estimates

Cost estimate for H.R. 5759, the Preventing Executive Overreach on Immigration Act of 2014 (December 3, 2014), www.cbo.gov/publication/49822.

Cost estimate for H.R. 15, the Border Security, Economic Opportunity, and Immigration Modernization Act (March 25, 2014), www.cbo.gov/publication/45206.

Cost estimate for H.R. 2131, the Supplying Knowledge-Based Immigrants and Lifting Levels of STEM Visas Act (SKILLS Visa Act) (March 12, 2014), www.cbo.gov/publication/45179.

Cost estimate for H.R. 2278, the Strengthen and Fortify Enforcement Act (December 5, 2013), www.cbo.gov/publication/44942.

Cost estimate for H.R. 1772, the Legal Workforce Act (December 17, 2013), www.cbo.gov/publication/44980.

Letter to the Honorable Patrick J. Leahy providing an estimate for S. 744, the Border Security, Economic Opportunity, and Immigration Modernization Act, as passed by the Senate on June 27, 2013 (July 3, 2013), www.cbo.gov/publication/44397.

Cost estimate for Senate Amendment 1183 to S. 744, the Border Security, Economic Opportunity, and Immigration Modernization Act (June 24, 2013), http://www.cbo.gov/publication/44372.

Cost estimate for S. 744, the Border Security, Economic Opportunity, and Immigration Modernization Act (June 18, 2013), www.cbo.gov/publication/44225.

Cost estimate for H.R. 6429, the STEM Jobs Act of 2012 (November 28, 2012), www.cbo.gov/publication/43740.

Cost estimate for H.R. 6497, the Development, Relief, and Education for Alien Minors Act of 2010 (December 8, 2010), www.cbo.gov/publication/21976.

Cost estimate for S. 3992, the Development, Relief, and Education for Alien Minors Act of 2010 (December 7, 2010), www.cbo.gov/publication/21973.

Cost estimate for Senate Amendment 1150 to S. 1348, the Comprehensive Immigration Reform Act of 2007 (June 4, 2007), www.cbo.gov/publication/18716.

Cost estimate for S. 2611, the Comprehensive Immigration Reform Act of 2006 (August 18, 2006), www.cbo.gov/publication/18065.

Glossary

Conditional permanent resident: A noncitizen who gains entrance to the United States because he or she has married a U.S. citizen or a lawful permanent resident, or has invested in a U.S. business. Status as a conditional permanent resident conveys the right to live and work in the United States for two years on a probationary basis. Conditional permanent residents have the same rights and responsibilities as permanent residents, but they must apply to remove the conditions placed on their permanent residence status after two years.

Deferred action: A process by which the Department of Homeland Security delays removal proceedings for unauthorized residents. Those who are approved for deferred action are considered lawfully present in the country but do not gain legal status.

Foreign born: Born outside the United States (or one of its territories) to parents who are not U.S. citizens.

Green card: A wallet-sized card showing that the bearer is a lawful permanent resident of the United States.

Lawful permanent resident (LPR): A noncitizen of the United States who is authorized to live, work, and study in the United States permanently. Such status is granted to immediate relatives of U.S. citizens (including spouses, minor children, and parents). It can also be granted on the basis of the following: family-sponsored preferences (for example, to extended family members, such as aunts or cousins); employment-based preferences; and diversity preferences.

The number of people who can be granted LPR status based on family-sponsored preferences, employment-based preferences, or diversity is subject to annual limits; by contrast, the number of people who can be granted LPR status each year because they are immediate relatives of U.S. citizens or for humanitarian reasons is unlimited. After becoming an LPR, a noncitizen immigrant receives a permanent resident card, commonly called a green card, which serves as proof of permission to live and work in the country.

Lawfully present: Foreign-born noncitizens who have met the requisite criteria for admission to the United States and, once admitted, have not stayed beyond the period originally authorized; or those who have current permission from the Citizenship and Immigration Services to stay or live in the United States.

Migrant: A person who moves to a country other than that of his or her usual residence, whether legally or illegally.

Native born: Born in the United States or one of its territories or, if born abroad, the child of at least one parent who is a U.S. citizen.

Naturalized citizen: A foreign-born person who has become a U.S. citizen by fulfilling requirements set forth in the Immigration and Nationality Act, including, in most cases, having resided in the United States for at least five years.

Noncitizen: Encompasses two categories of foreign-born people—those who are authorized to live and work in the United States either temporarily or permanently (see "conditional permanent resident," "lawful permanent resident," "temporary resident or visitor," "temporary worker," and "refugee or asylum-seeker"); and those who are not authorized to live or work in the United States (see "unauthorized resident").

Qualified alien: As defined in the Personal Responsibility and Work Opportunity Reconciliation Act of 1996, a subset of noncitizens that are eligible for public benefit programs, such as the Supplemental Nutrition Assistance Program and Medicaid. Qualified aliens primarily include LPRs, refugees, and people who have been granted asylum. Most other categories of noncitizens—including temporary residents and visitors as well as all unauthorized residents—are not considered qualified aliens.

Refugee or asylum-seeker: A person who has been persecuted in his or her home country or who has a well-founded fear of persecution in that country on the basis of race, religion, nationality, membership in a particular social group, or political opinion. Such individuals who are outside of the United States apply for refugee status. Those who are inside of the United States apply for asylum.

Removal: The expulsion of a foreign-born individual from the United States if he or she is found to be inadmissible at a port of entry or otherwise in violation of U.S. immigration laws. An inadmissible individual is a person who seeks entry but does not meet the criteria of the Immigration and Nationality Act.

Temporary resident or visitor: A noncitizen who is admitted to the United States with a temporary visa or who is allowed to enter the country without a visa. People in those categories include visitors who are in the United States for short periods and temporary residents who are in the United States for longer, although still time-limited, stays.

Temporary worker: A noncitizen who is admitted to the United States with a temporary visa for purposes of time-limited employment.

Unauthorized resident: A noncitizen of the United States who is in the country without legal authorization. This category includes people who enter the country illegally and those who enter with valid visas but overstay their authorized time in the country. In this report, the category also encompasses those formerly unauthorized residents who have been approved for deferred action; they are lawfully present without legal status for the duration of their deferral.

U.S. visa: A permit allowing the bearer to apply for entry to the United States under a certain classification. Examples of those visa classifications include: student (F), visitor (B), and temporary worker (H). The Department of State is responsible for issuing visas at U.S. embassies and consulates outside of the United States. A visa does not grant the bearer the right to enter the United States. Officials with the Department of Homeland Security's Customs and Border Protection determine whether an individual can be admitted to the United States at a port of entry. A person may be denied entry by an official because he or she lacks proper documentation, because of public health or security concerns, or for other reasons.

List of Tables and Figures

About This Document

This Congressional Budget Office (CBO) report describes the factors the agency considers when estimating the budgetary effects of proposed changes to immigration policy. In keeping with CBO's mandate to provide objective, impartial analysis, the report contains no recommendations.

Melissa Merrell, of CBO's Budget Analysis Division, and Jonathan Schwabish, formerly of CBO's Health, Retirement, and Long-Term Analysis Division, wrote the report under the guidance of Peter Fontaine and Linda Bilheimer. Nabeel Alsalam, Christina Hawley Anthony, Lisa Ramirez Branum, Sheila Dacey, Wendy Edelberg, Kathleen FitzGerald, Mark Grabowicz, Janet Holtzblatt, Justin Humphrey, Geena Kim, Sarah Masi, Sam Pampenfuss, David Rafferty, Kyle Redfield, Felix Reichling, Emily Stern, and Robert Stewart, all of CBO, as well as Kirstin Blom, Chris Murphy, and Vi Nguyen, formerly of CBO, provided helpful comments.

Rakesh Kochhar of Pew Hispanic Center, Alex Nowrasteh of the Cato Institute, Ruth Wasem of the Congressional Research Service, and Jessica Zuckerman of the Heritage Foundation reviewed the report. The assistance of external reviewers implies no responsibility for the final product, which rests solely with CBO.

Robert Sunshine reviewed the report, Loretta Lettner edited it, and Maureen Costantino and Jeanine Rees prepared it for publication. The report is available on CBO's website (www.cbo.gov/publication/49868).

Douglas W. Elmendorf
Director

January 2015

www.ingramcontent.com/pod-product-compliance
Lightning Source LLC
Chambersburg PA
CBHW080633290526
45790CB00007B/3045